# FROM GHETTO TO GUERRILLA

## Memoir Of A Jewish Resistance Fighter

## BY SAMUEL LATO

PREEMINENT PUBLISHING INCORPORATED
FLORIDA

Copyright © 2006 by Samuel Lato

Published in the United States by Preeminent Publishing Incorporated, Florida. All rights reserved. No part of this work may be reproduced or transmitted in any form or by any means, electronic or mechanical, including photocopying, recording, or by any information storage and retrieval system, without the prior written permission of the publisher.

First Edition

LIBRARY OF CONGRESS CATALOGING–IN–PUBLICATION DATA IS AVAILABLE UPON REQUEST

LATO, SAMUEL

**From Ghetto To Guerrilla:
Memoir Of A Jewish Resistance Fighter**

Library of Congress Control Number: 2006930180

Book design by Jim Johnston / ImageBlast Inc.

Preeminent books may be purchased from the website www.PREEMINENTPUBLISHING.com or by writing to the publisher at 4371 Northlake Boulevard, Suite#369, Palm Beach Gardens, Florida 33410

PRINTED IN CHINA

I S B N
9780977762194
0-9777621-9-X

# FROM GHETTO TO GUERRILLA

# DEDICATION

I dedicate this book to the memory
of my family; I miss and mourn them:

— MY PARENTS —
SARA PORTNOFF LATO
AND
EDWARD LATO

— MY 10-YEAR-OLD BROTHER —
JACKOB

THE 39 AUNTS, UNCLES
AND COUSINS LATO

THE 6 MEMBERS OF
THE FAMILY PORTNOFF
AND
THE 13,000 JEWS OF BARANOWICZE,
ALL MASSACRED BY
THE BARBARIC NAZI REGIME

---

I bequeath this story and the memory
of those who perished to:

— MY BELOVED SON —
EDWARD LATO

And to my cherished grandchildren:
SCOTT LATO
BRETT LATO
JENNIFER LATO

# CONTENTS

INTRODUCTION . . . . . . . . . . . . . . . . . . . . . . . . . . . . . . *page* x

**PART 1 – MY FAMILY** . . . . . . . . . . . . . . . . . . . . . . . . . . . . . 1
   *Poland 1925–1939* . . . . . . . . . . . . . . . . . . . . . . . . . . . . . . 4
   *Belarus 1939–1941* . . . . . . . . . . . . . . . . . . . . . . . . . . . . . 14

**PART 2 – THE GERMANS INVADE** . . . . . . . . . . . . . . . . . . . . 19
   *The Bombing Begins – June 22, 1941* . . . . . . . . . . . . . . . . . . . . 20
   *Occupation Of Baranowicze – June 30, 1941* . . . . . . . . . . . . . . . 25
   *Roundups* . . . . . . . . . . . . . . . . . . . . . . . . . . . . . . . . . . . . 30
   *Living With death* . . . . . . . . . . . . . . . . . . . . . . . . . . . . . . . 36

**PART 3 – THE GHETTO** . . . . . . . . . . . . . . . . . . . . . . . . . . . 43
   *The Ghetto Is Established – Rosh Hashanah 1941* . . . . . . . . . . . . 44
   *The Ghetto Is Sealed – Christmas 1941* . . . . . . . . . . . . . . . . . . 53
   *Life In The Ghetto* . . . . . . . . . . . . . . . . . . . . . . . . . . . . . . . 61
   *The First Slaughter – Purim 1942* . . . . . . . . . . . . . . . . . . . . . 69
   *Resistance* . . . . . . . . . . . . . . . . . . . . . . . . . . . . . . . . . . . . 74
   *The Second Slaughter – Rosh Hashanah 1942* . . . . . . . . . . . . . . 82
   *Escape – October 9, 1942* . . . . . . . . . . . . . . . . . . . . . . . . . . 90

**PART 4 – THE PARTISANS** . . . . . . . . . . . . . . . . . . . . . . . . 93
   *The 10th Lock* . . . . . . . . . . . . . . . . . . . . . . . . . . . . . . . . . 96
   *Partisan Camp – Living In The Forest* . . . . . . . . . . . . . . . . . . 106
   *Misha And The Making of A Partisan* . . . . . . . . . . . . . . . . . . 114
   *Wooden Guns And Food Missions – Winter 1942* . . . . . . . . . . . 119
   *Making More Noise* . . . . . . . . . . . . . . . . . . . . . . . . . . . . . 125

**PART 4** – THE PARTISANS *(continued)*
   *The Final Slaughter – Christmas 1942* . . . . . . . . . . . . . . . . . . . . . 135
   *Guerrilla Warfare – Spring 1943* . . . . . . . . . . . . . . . . . . . . . . . . . 139
   *Victory At Stalingrad – February 2, 1943* . . . . . . . . . . . . . . . . . . 145
   *The Dirty Thirty* . . . . . . . . . . . . . . . . . . . . . . . . . . . . . . . . . . . . . 148
   *Meeting In The Forest* . . . . . . . . . . . . . . . . . . . . . . . . . . . . . . . . 155
   *Air Drops* . . . . . . . . . . . . . . . . . . . . . . . . . . . . . . . . . . . . . . . . . 161
   *Warsaw Ghetto Uprising – Passover 1943* . . . . . . . . . . . . . . . . . 166
   *Hatred And Revenge* . . . . . . . . . . . . . . . . . . . . . . . . . . . . . . . . . 170
   *Hope For Rescue* . . . . . . . . . . . . . . . . . . . . . . . . . . . . . . . . . . . 174
   *Missions 1 – Toll Of War* . . . . . . . . . . . . . . . . . . . . . . . . . . . . . .180
   *The Little Green Forest* . . . . . . . . . . . . . . . . . . . . . . . . . . . . . . .185
   *Missions 2 – Take No Prisoners* . . . . . . . . . . . . . . . . . . . . . . . . 188
   *Partisan Wedding – Love In The Forest* . . . . . . . . . . . . . . . . . . . 194
   *Liberation – July 22, 1944* . . . . . . . . . . . . . . . . . . . . . . . . . . . . 197

**PART 5** – THE RUSSIAN ARMY . . . . . . . . . . . . . . . . . . . . . . . . . . .203
   *The Russian Front – The Mother of War* . . . . . . . . . . . . . . . . . . 204
   *The Big Push* . . . . . . . . . . . . . . . . . . . . . . . . . . . . . . . . . . . . . . 212
   *Dodging A Final Bullet* . . . . . . . . . . . . . . . . . . . . . . . . . . . . . . .217
   *End Of War, But Not Prejudice* . . . . . . . . . . . . . . . . . . . . . . . . . 222
   *Homeward Bound* . . . . . . . . . . . . . . . . . . . . . . . . . . . . . . . . . .224
   *Return To Baranowicze* . . . . . . . . . . . . . . . . . . . . . . . . . . . . . .225

EPILOGUE . . . . . . . . . . . . . . . . . . . . . . . . . . . . . . . . . . . . . . . . . . . . 230
AFTERWORD . . . . . . . . . . . . . . . . . . . . . . . . . . . . . . . . . . . . . . . . . .232

LATO PHOTO COLLECTION
   *Selected Photos From Samuel Lato's Album* . . . . . . . . . . . . . . . . 235

# Illustrations

*Map of Poland Circa 1937* .............. 2

*Map of Poland after German Invasion 1939* .. 26

*Map of Eastern Europe after German Invasion of Russia 1941* ...................... 27

*Map of the Baranowicze ghetto, 1943* ...... 60

*Map of Partisan activity 1942-1944* ........ 94

# Photographs

*Edward Lato* ......................... 6
*Sara Lato* ........................... 7
*Samuel, Sara and Jackob Lato* .......... 11
*Aunt Rosa and Samuel* ................ 13

*Sara Lato's letter – A mother writes to her son* ........... 178

*Genia Wishnia Lato 1938* ......................... 200
*Samuel Lato, day after liberation* .................. 200
*Samuel is recruited into the Russian army 1944* ........ 201
*Genia and Samuel in Baranowicze after the war* ........ 227

*Monument to Jewish victims in Baranowicze* ............ 228
*Survivors in Baranowicze* ........................ 229

*Samuel Lato, the author, today* ...................... 233

I obtained this book from a stamp collector in 1945 and converted it into a Photo Album; a curious repository in which I placed the pictures of my family that I was able to recover. Family friends who had fled to Moscow early in the war were able to provide me with many of these pictures.

While waiting for permission to immigrate to America, I spent many hours decorating the borders of each and every picture with a design drawn by hand. The photographs contained within this book come from that Album.

# INTRODUCTION

The Jews did not go quietly. We Jews did not passively walk to our deaths in cramped ghettos and barren death camps and putrid, shallow graves dug by our Jewish brothers. Resistance, both peaceful and fierce, was waged by rabbis, senior adults and men, women and children alike.

I know. I was there.

I was one of them.

Was smuggling food, medicine and even an extra pair of socks into the ghettos past surly, glaring guards – all at the risk of certain death – not resistance enough? Was making defective shells for the German army not a calculated act, saving thousands of lives? Or the acts by the freedom fighters in the forest?

The Jews sought revenge against their Nazi enemies. The Jews wrought death and destruction to those who had killed their families, raped their mothers, wives and daughters and wounded their very souls.

The Jews took up arms.

I know. I was one of them.

I made my own boots. I lived off cabbage roots and raw potatoes in the forests. Trained by Russian officers, emboldened by anger, fear, hatred and sorrow, I made it through by the dint of youth, courage, skill, the will to survive and just plain, dumb luck.

Yes, the Jews fought back.

I know. I was one of them.

My entire family of 45 people – including my father, my mother, my brother, my aunts, my uncles and my cousins – was wiped out in the Holocaust: murdered; exterminated by the Germans and their collaborators.

The people I shared holidays, weddings and funerals with. Who gave me gifts on my birthday. Who pinched my cheeks until they were rosy red, and then pinched them some more. Who ate at our dinner table, smoked in our living room and complimented my mother's cooking. Who winked at me, laughed with good humor at my jokes and gave me nickels for ice cream. The people who filled our family photo album with smiles and frowns and the clothes and hairstyles of the day, who were supposed to go on for generations and generations, filling the town records with the name Lato for centuries to come, all gone. Forever.

No more birthdays. No more pinched cheeks. No more nickels for ice cream. No more photos for our family album.

Just me.

I am the only survivor.

This is my story.

— Samuel Lato

# Part 1
# My Family

"OPINIONS FOUNDED ON PREJUDICE ARE ALWAYS SUSTAINED WITH THE GREATEST VIOLENCE."

– Jewish proverb

European Borders Circa 1937

# POLAND

*1925-1939*

My name is Samuel Lato. I am eighty-one years old. I am a survivor of the Holocaust. But before I was labeled a Jew, before I was labeled a Holocaust survivor, before Hitler, before the Nazis, before the brown shirts, before the yellow stars, before I lived through hell – before all that – I was just another baby boy cooing softly in his mother's arms.

I was born on February 24, 1925, in Baranowicze, a small town in Poland bordering the powerful Soviet Union; a beautiful town abloom with greenery, flowers, trees and orchards. There were 25,000 people, 5,000 of them Jews, living in this quiet, peaceful town before the war. Until I was sixteen I grew up surrounded by a loving family, plenty of aunts, uncles and cousins and all of my childhood friends, safe in my little town of Baranowicze, my home for as long as I could remember. A place with two movie theaters and wide open streets. A place with shops: barbers, bakers and cobblers. A place with a stadium for soccer games and graduations.

But war was soon to find the family Lato and me in our quiet, peaceful, little town.

---

The *Shoah* did not start with Auschwitz, Treblinka and Buchenwald. The tragedy began way before: slowly, quietly, stealthily. It began with Hitler feeding poisonous lies and hate to the people, maliciously presenting Jews to the world as misfits, as sub-humans. It spread like a contagion, in the air and over the radio, on the tongues and furtive glances between fair-haired gentiles as Jews innocently passed by. It sat next to you in beer halls, stood alongside you at the baker's and hissed behind you in the classroom.

Before the Second World War, between 1928 and 1939, my family lived in Warsaw, the capital of Poland. My father supported my mother, my brother and me with a series of accounting jobs that went smoothly until his employers learned he was Jewish. Then he was always politely asked to resign. It was very hard for a Jewish professional man to find a job with a company and keep it. I learned early on that war could be waged without shiny black boots, sharp-edged swastikas and hot slugs of lead. I watched my father trudge home from another forced resignation, another lost job, another missing paycheck, only because he was a Jew. Even though my father looked and spoke like a gentile, he was not successful in passing as one. It was hard to fool a Jew hater.

I was three years old when we moved to Warsaw in 1928. My father had been offered an excellent position as a manager of a large bank by the name of Lombard. He had graduated from the prestigious University of Warsaw as an accountant. He spoke fluent Polish, Russian, and German and fairly good English and Yiddish. My father had seven brothers and one sister, all born and raised in Warsaw, all graduates of the University of Warsaw.

In those days my grandfather was very rich. He and his brother managed the tailor shop in the Warsaw Regional Court of the High Prince, the brother of the Russian tsar. My grandfather's clientele were the elite of Warsaw and, even though he was one of the richest men in the city, he was still a commoner. Because of that, when my grandmother Baroness Von Milhowse from Silesia, Germany married him, she lost her title. In 1914 during the First World War, my grandfather lost his fortune, just like most of his friends. He had sold his real estate holdings for cash, but in a short time the money was worthless, just paper.

My father and mother,
Edward and Sara Lato, Baranowicze, 1923

When we first moved to Warsaw we lived with my grandparents in their apartment. I remember two tenants in the building: Mania Kotlitzka, owner of the grocery store, and Goldfarb the tailor. In 1929 we moved to an apartment of our own.

That year I started school. The kids called me "Munio," my nickname, a shortened version of Samuel. I attended a Jewish public school. Christian kids attended Christian public schools and private schools had mixed attendance. There was minimal contact between us.

The first week my mother walked me to school to show me the way and teach me how to cross the street. I remember walking by Krasinsky Park, and that it took about thirty minutes to get to school. The following week, carrying a stick, I walked by myself but in a group with other Jews. We were fearful of gentiles.

In 1931 when I turned six, the bank that my father was managing was sold to a company from Switzerland. Again, when they found out that he was Jewish he was forced to resign. When I heard that, I was devastated; feeling his pain, I became sick to my stomach. To me, my father was my god and my mother, my angel.

To my sorrow we had to give up our nice apartment and sublet a room and share the common areas with the original tenant. My father found another job as a manager of Hazet, a Swiss chocolate company. On Fridays he would bring home a bag of mixed chocolates that I enjoyed. In our next move we again had our own apartment. The building had a large courtyard with trees, shrubs, flowers and a few benches. I became friends with a nice kid, Berek Weisfeld, and we played hide and seek, cowboys and Indians and other games like soccer, ping-pong and chess. We lived there about a year, until the company found out that my father was Jewish and again he was asked to resign.

Throughout all our moves my father's brothers, Max, Carol,

Ludwig and Joseph, always lived in the same Jewish neighborhood. My mother was religious; she kept kosher and blessed the Sabbath candles. When I was eight years old, my brother Jackob was born. We called him "Kubek," Polish for "little one," little Jackob. Whenever my Aunt Rosa visited us in Warsaw she always stayed with us in our one room. She slept on the floor even though she could well afford a fancy hotel. She was always happy to be with us. She would come four or five times a year for two weeks at a time.

My father's next job was managing the office of Sportsoap, a large company where he worked for a year until they, too, found out he was Jewish. It was always devastating to me and I got sick every time my father lost a job. I was very attached to him.

With the last job loss my father decided to stop looking and instead became a peddler, selling cosmetics. His well-to-do cousins in Warsaw started recommending him to their wealthy friends and with hard work he built up a clientele.

After the second grade I went to a school closer to home. I was a good student, artistically inclined, imaginative and with uncommon common sense. I was good with my hands and made toys for my brother and me, creating new and interesting things. A "grown-up" ten year old, I played chess with the big guys – my father, my grandfather and my Uncle Joseph, who played professionally. We usually played in our apartment and most of the time my mother would prepare cheese blintzes and coffee for lunch.

In the new school I became friends with a kid whose father owned a machine shop that made hinges. They hired outside people to assemble hinges for one cent apiece. I was not bashful and asked if I could have some hinges to work on. They gave me a hundred. It took me three hours to assemble them. The next time they gave me two hundred. In those days in Poland, two zlotys was a lot of money (one zloty equaled around eleven cents.). I assembled hinges for the next three years. It made me proud to earn additional money for my family.

---

I loved Baranowicze, my town. I loved the orchards, trees, flowers and the open spaces. Most of my summer and winter vacations I stayed there with my Aunt Rosa and Uncle Noahm. I had many cousins and friends. They treated me like an aristocrat from the big city. My aunt was very proud of me, for the way I talked and behaved. She loved me like a mother and so did her children: Lutek, Frieda, Minar, Genia and Simar. I had no idea then that the girls were not my real cousins because she loved them all like her own. But they were her stepchildren. She herself had only one son, Lutek. She married my uncle Noahm Dubrowkin when his four girls were little, only one, two, three and four years old. It was while sitting *shiva* for my uncle in 1938 that I would find out about my cousins. Uncle Noahm was a good man.

During the third and fourth grades, my mother was the one raising Kubek and me. My father would leave the house at 8 a.m. and not return until after 8 p.m. We were poor, had little money, but we were rich in spirit. My father carried a suitcase full of cosmetics, walking from door to door, from customer to customer.

I was craving to have a scooter, but we could not afford one, so I decided to make one myself. It turned out almost perfect. All the kids in the courtyard were jealous and wanted to have one just like mine. This was a big achievement for a kid my age and my parents were very proud of me.

We were a multilingual family. My parents spoke Russian to each other. I spoke Polish to my mother, which she understood well but did not speak, and she spoke Russian or Yiddish to me.

Me at 10 years of age with my mother Sara and little brother Jackob in Baranowicze, 1935

My father and I spoke Polish to each other. As a family we communicated and understood each other very well and had an almost perfect relationship.

In November 1937 my father won the Polish state lottery of 22,500 zlotys. At the time this was a large amount, about $2,500. Overnight we became rich. The first thing my father did was run to the bakery to buy a cake for the family and, for me, a *boyaderka*, my favorite, a special chocolate rum cake.

After winning the lottery our lives changed completely. First my father started a regular cosmetics business and hired another salesman. At that moment everything was working in our favor. My father, a hardworking man who never gave up, was making a good life for all of us. To him, his family was everything; his life. I always hoped that I would inherit all of his qualities. My parents rented a nice three-bedroom apartment with a kitchen and a bathroom. We even had a balcony. Life became more pleasant.

In the spring of 1938 the Jewish Federation of Warsaw opened a Jewish high school and trade school in one. This was the only school like it in Poland: four hours of regular school and four hours of trade school, eight hours a day six days a week. They had 1,000 applications, but room for only 100 students, 50 in a class. They awarded 10 scholarships. I was very fortunate to receive a partial scholarship. My Aunt Rosa's gift was a promise to pay my tuition until I graduated. I was so happy and excited that I could not stop talking about it.

The trade school had a contest where students could plan and produce any item they wanted, with the school providing the necessary materials. I elected to make a pair of ice skates. I had never had any of my own. My professor told me that I had made a bad choice, but it did not stop me. I made the ice skates and won the contest. First prize was a full scholarship for the rest of the three years. My professor complimented me and confessed that he could not believe that a kid had created such a well-built

Me (center) with my aunt, Rosa Dubrowkin (right), and a close family friend, Fella Epstein. Barmitzvah Day February 24, 1938.

product. I thanked him. My parents said they did not know how to express how much they appreciated me. It was two weeks after my bar mitzvah. I was thirteen. I was in seventh heaven.

School went by quickly. After I completed my second year, I went to stay in Baranowicze as I always did, to spend the summer at my Aunt Rosa's. It was 1939.

It would be in Baranowicze where the war would find me.

I would never finish school in Warsaw.

I would never visit Warsaw again..

# BELARUS

*1939-1941*

My summer days with my aunt in Baranowicze passed in a blur of green grass and lemonade, but reports of Hitler's advancing armies filled the airwaves, newspapers and the talk in the coffee shops. Our hopes were that Germany would not make it to Poland. I grew restless and worried about my family and our apartment in Warsaw.

World War II began on September 1, 1939, and our worst fears were confirmed. It took the Germans only 17 days to capture the western part of Poland. It happened fast, viciously and without resistance. The Germans gave it a name, *blitzkrieg*, or "lightning war." I was fourteen years old.

In short catastrophic order Germany invaded Warsaw and the war in Poland was over. The Soviet Union and Germany split Poland, with Germany occupying the west and the Russians the east, which was then annexed to Belarus.

During the bombardment of Warsaw our apartment was destroyed in a bone-splintering blink of an eye. The baker, the cobbler and the butcher all lost their shops and their livelihoods that fateful day. With the sweep of tanks and the crunching of glass under stiff black boots, the Germans entered the city and marched unchallenged up the middle of the streets. The writing was on the wall. While not as widespread as it would later become, the persecution of the Jews had begun. Thinly-veiled threats and whispered stories of violence that had already occurred began to make their way back to my family as they searched to find a roof that wasn't still smoldering or already caved in.

Hundreds of thousands of Jewish people escaped to East Poland, to Belarus, our ally.

My father decided to do the same. So he, my mother and my brother Jackob, then six, left Warsaw and headed east, back to our family home of Baranowicze, that peaceful town the family had left in pursuit of a better job for my father. It was over two hundred treacherous miles – a distance difficult and long, filled with uncertainty, doubt and no guarantee of safety. My father, though strong, was unaccustomed to such grueling physical exertion. My mother, a housewife, and my brother fared worse. It would take them over three weeks to reach us.

My aunt and I awaited their arrival anxiously, our ears glued to the door. Reports from neighbors and friends were troubling. Rumors were everywhere. The dull, heavy threat of violence crackled in the air like heat lightning. With no way of communicating, we had no idea whether they were healthy, sick or worse.

But the future – and hope – was in the east. Only death resided in the west.

And so they walked: an accountant, a housewife and one frightened little boy. They were like many Jews in the same situation: average, everyday people who had been thrust into an extraordinary situation. They adapted, improvised and walked. It was all they could do. War had entered our lives and crept heavy and burdensome onto our shoulders. The childish concerns and safety of yesterday were squashed.

My family finally arrived the second week of October 1939. It was a bittersweet reunion: hugs, kisses and many tears. This time, though, my father easily found a job in the Russian state government. As a graduate of Warsaw University's prestigious School of Accounting – and fluent in Russian – his skills were suddenly in high demand as the occupying forces of the Soviet Union took up residence in local offices, parlors and halls.

Slowly, hesitantly, like dogs that had been kicked, we started a new life. We settled down in a house my parents owned and began making hopeful plans for an uncertain future. My father's seven brothers and their families had also escaped from Warsaw and moved in temporarily with my Aunt Rosa, who had a large house. After they found jobs they moved into apartments of their own. With war-torn Warsaw behind us, we settled down. For a while life in our town was quiet and peaceful, even as pleasant as it was before the war.

The fleeting days of that summer passed almost serenely except for the growing concern over Germany's strength as it bit off and chewed up parts of Poland. Too soon summer ended and I started school again. Things were different with the Russians in charge of the school system. We had only three months in which to learn the Russian language, after which classes would be held only in Russian, now the official language. It was very difficult to learn an entire language in such a short time, but I had a head start because my parents spoke Russian.

That year a choir was organized at school and I eagerly signed up for it, my young, clear voice joining with those of my schoolmates in innocence and praise of our newfound safety and security. In the springtime of 1940 we won first place in the Belarus Region Musical Olympiad. I joined the city choir as well.

I was fifteen, a basso singing with a choir of forty: young, old, rich, poor, short and tall. We felt safe. We were singing. We were alive.

Life went on like that for almost 2 years. I played sports – soccer, ping-pong, volleyball – whatever I could to stay busy and ignore the growing concerns my parents shared ever so quietly at the dinner table each night.

Because of my artistic inclination, the school's social director enlisted me as her helper and I worked on decorations for special events. I was also on the school's gymnastics team, which placed second in the finals of the National Competition held in Minsk, the capital of Belarus.

We were busy kids with no time to create any problems for our parents or the school. The Russians also established in each city a "House of National Art." It was here that anybody could come, join and have the opportunity to participate and learn dancing, singing, acting, painting or writing.

I was a boy, fourteen, fifteen and then sixteen, busy with all my activities. And girls! I attended all the social events our school had to offer. I went to movies. I dated, joked around with friends and drank lemonade in the shade. Life was good, simple, pleasant and safe. My father had a great job, manager for all the movie theaters in the Baranowicze region. My mother took care of the house. My brother stumbled on my coattails.

Then, before I knew it, school was over. It was time for me to graduate.

But, abruptly, I would be forced to graduate from more than school.

Part 2
# The Germans Invade

"HATRED IS A TERRIBLE THING, BOTH TO THOSE WHO ARE HATED, AND TO THOSE WHO HATE."

– Samuel Lato

# THE BOMBING BEGINS

*JUNE 22, 1941*

On the day before we were to receive our diplomas, my friends and I had a graduation party to celebrate the momentous occasion. It was a festive affair, full of brimming pride, cocky showmanship and naïve innocence. But not just for the children: our parents got involved as well. I think they understood that the time of innocence was ticking away and that they should enjoy a little of it before it was gone forever.

My father, especially, got into the spirit of the occasion. In a crowded kitchen full of laughter and mirth, he cheerfully offered to help me prepare a fancy "cocktail," a very special drink for a very special occasion. I remember he cooked strong coffee. I can still smell it. He mixed it with thick, whole cream and a lot of sugar. Then, when my mother wasn't looking, he would wink at me while he added some vodka. He called it a "liqueur."

I had never felt so grown up. He had never looked so proud.

We had a wonderful time at the party that evening. We were but children in more ways than one. I remember our only thought was that we were happy, very happy, to be done with school. Summer was here. That was uppermost on our young minds. On this night, we thought of good things, happy things, youthful things. We sang, danced, talked, told jokes, flirted and played childish games.

When the party was over, we young strapping fellows, good

gentlemen all, walked our girlfriends safely to their front doors, then went straight home. We said goodnight to each other as happy and giddy children, with the entire summer stretching before us. We were sixteen, young and carefree, had our whole lives ahead of us and were protected by the strong Russian army.

That night I went to sleep immediately, eager to get plenty of rest for the big day tomorrow: graduation day. We were to stand in line, hear speeches and applause and receive our official crisp and starched diplomas, which our proud mothers were waiting to frame and hang in places of prominence on living room walls crowded with other family photos.

When I walked out of my house early that morning to go to graduation, I was stopped by an imposing yet somber Russian policeman who told me quite sternly that I couldn't go anyplace – not to the stadium, not to the theater, not to the drugstore, not up the street. We were at war with Germany. According to what he had been told by his superiors, the Russians expected German warplanes to begin bombing the city – my city – at any moment. To avoid panic in the streets, the police had orders to keep us in our houses, behind closed doors.

I rushed inside to inform my family and we crowded by the window, in the front doorway, anywhere we could to hear the latest news as it swept down the street.

At 4 in the morning on Sunday, June 22, 1941, the German armies crossed the borders of the Soviet Union, and Hitler's devoted troops effectively started invading Russia. Before the sun rose that fateful morning, Russian soldiers were losing their lives by the hundreds, ground underfoot by the crushing German army.

No graduation. No speeches. No applause. No diplomas.

As that fearful graduation day wore on, the police advised us to dig trenches in our backyards, hunker down and cover our heads in case there was bombing. This fear was not unfounded. We all knew that our town was right next to a railroad, a main line to the east that went directly to Moscow.

I was surprised at how calmly and efficiently my father went about this task of digging trenches. But I shouldn't have been. After all, while I had been enjoying a carefree summer with my aunt in Baranowicze, my family had already been through this in Warsaw. They had seen the destruction; they knew what bombs could do. They had already lost one home and were not willing to risk their lives as well. Up went the flower beds, down went the tomato beds. We dug the trenches as deep as we could. Then we hunkered down and waited.

The Germans waited, too. They waited until 4 p.m. the next day to bomb our peaceful, little town of Baranowicze. In that late afternoon sky I counted 9 planes. The German bombers blotted out the sky with ominous presence and deafening roar. The ground shook long before the first bomb fell.

This was the first time in my life that I had heard bombs explode. They were deafening, frightening and bone-rattling. I thought my teeth would break each time one fell. The shriek as they fell through the air was almost as deafening as the ear-shattering roar when they hit the ground. A slight whistling, a deafening hum and an eerie silence just before impact.

The destruction was catastrophic and complete. In one short hour, 50 to 60 bombs were dropped on my childhood home. One bomb landed on our neighbor's house. Our neighbor's! The house was demolished completely. Looking at it afterward, the splinters that once were roof beams, the shards that once were windows, the lint that once were drapes, it was hard to believe that nobody had been killed.

The next day the planes filled the air once again for a second, more thorough round of bombing. This time I counted 27 planes crowding the blue Polish sky, each one proceeding mercilessly along its path, opening big bombardier doors and dropping endless bombs that whistled and screamed upon our tiny town. They destroyed the radio station, damaged the railroad station and obliterated entire neighborhoods.

After all that destruction, after over two days of intense carpet bombing, 100s of bombs, I was amazed to hear that not one person in all of Baranowicze had been killed. I am sure that those trenches had saved our lives.

When the bombing stopped what was demolished was useless, what was standing was wobbly and what was undamaged would quickly be overrun by German soldiers. Out of the trenches we came, desperately surveying the damage, checking on loved ones and our homes. Our town would never be the same.

In the unsettling peace and quiet that temporarily followed our *blitzkrieg*, our own "lightning war," my father and uncle wasted no time planning for our future. They talked earnestly about running away from Baranowicze to avoid being captured by the advancing German army. They had heard stories about what had happened to the Jews left behind in Warsaw after the Germans invaded. The harsh restrictions, the new laws, the prohibitions, the rumors of violence and death. Were the peaceful Jews of Baranowicze next?

My family seemed to think so. After four days of deliberations, of arguing, of worrying, we decided to leave for Minsk. We packed our bags carefully, taking the clothes and food we needed for the long journey ahead.

On Thursday morning, June 26, 1941, we left Baranowicze and started walking east, toward Minsk. The summer weather was very nice that day, but we were dressed heavily – each wearing two pairs of pants, two shirts and a winter coat – so our bags would be lighter.

After a while we got hot and tired and started walking more slowly. Then slower and slower until we were doing little more then shuffling under the heavy June heat. The luggage and thick winter clothes made our arms and legs stiff like snowmen. It took us all day to walk ten miles. In our travels that day we never saw one single Russian soldier. For so long now on the streets of Baranowicze, in the meeting halls, on the nearby airfield, along the railroad tracks, the presence of the friendly Russian army had been a comfort to us. Now they were nowhere to be seen. We were on our own.

We suspected that the Germans were closing in on us. After a short rest and a nap, we started walking again, careful to walk only in the dark. We had no idea where the Germans might be or how long we had, so we pushed on, all of us stiff and sore, the children, too, carrying as many bags as they could.

The next day, struggling to outpace the Nazis, we walked another ten miles.

But the German army finally caught up to us and threatened us with guns. We turned around and started walking back home.

Later that evening, as we retraced our steps, we got caught in a crossfire between the Germans and the Russians.

Instinctively we fell to our bellies while the two armies fired at one another, bullets whizzing right past our heads and driving our faces deeper and deeper into the dewy grass. The firefight lasted only an hour, until the Russians gave up and ran away, but with our faces pressed into the earth it felt like an eternity. We were in shock, extremely confused, our ears ringing from the deafening gunfire. It was a miracle that none of us was injured or killed that night.

It was also a bitter sign of things to come.

My father wanted us to run from the area as quickly as possible. So we ignored our aching muscles, our grumbling stomachs, our chafing blisters and our sweat. We walked all night and all of the next day, trudging on endlessly with only a few brief stops and reached Baranowicze on June 30, 1941.

# OCCUPATION OF BARANOWICZE

*June 30, 1941*

Surprisingly the German military did not bother us when we arrived within the ravaged city limits. They never stopped us or asked any questions about who we were or where we were going. We returned to our home unmolested, cleaned up, unpacked and waited anxiously for "the other shoe to drop," as my mother always said.

For the next two days everything was quiet.

But we knew it wouldn't last. Already the air in the Jewish neighborhood was heavy with dread and fear. We were scared, waiting for disaster to strike. And it did.

With the Russian army driven out, our protectors were gone. Shortly after bombing and invading my peaceful hometown of Baranowicze, the occupying German forces began their unrelenting campaign of shame, agony and terror against *my* people: the Jewish people.

In the first few days of the occupation the Germans swiftly issued restrictive new rules against the Jews. The first law they enforced was that Jews must wear a white band a little less than four inches wide displaying a blue Star of David on the right sleeve of inner and outer garments.

No more checking papers, no more listening for accents, no more guessing, just a simple white band across the right arm.

Next the Germans enacted a law that Jews must walk in the middle of the street. We were no longer allowed to walk on *our* sidewalks with the rest of the good citizens of Baranowicze. The sidewalks of our hometown, shop-lined and familiar, paved and

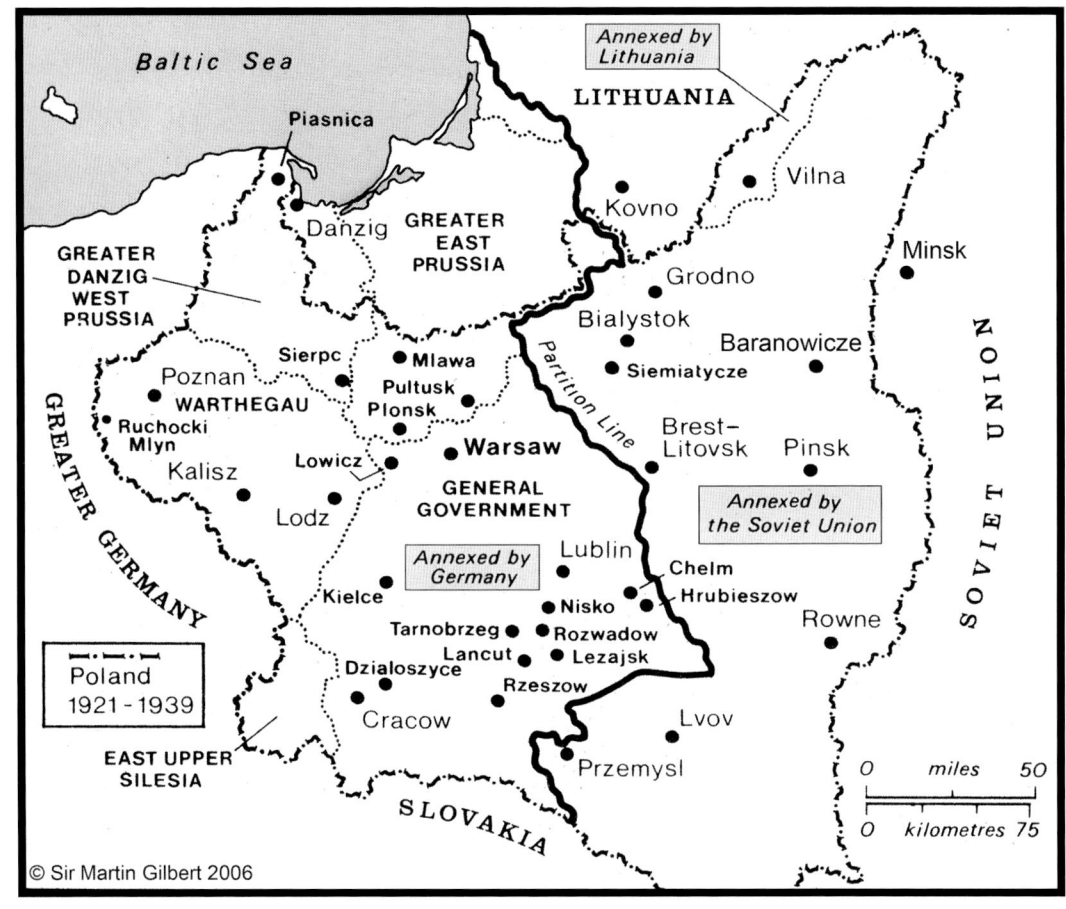

**ABOVE**
The partition of Poland after the German Invasion, 1939. World War II begins.

**RIGHT**
The 1941 German Invasion of the Soviet Union showing boundaries of Eastern Europe in 1942.

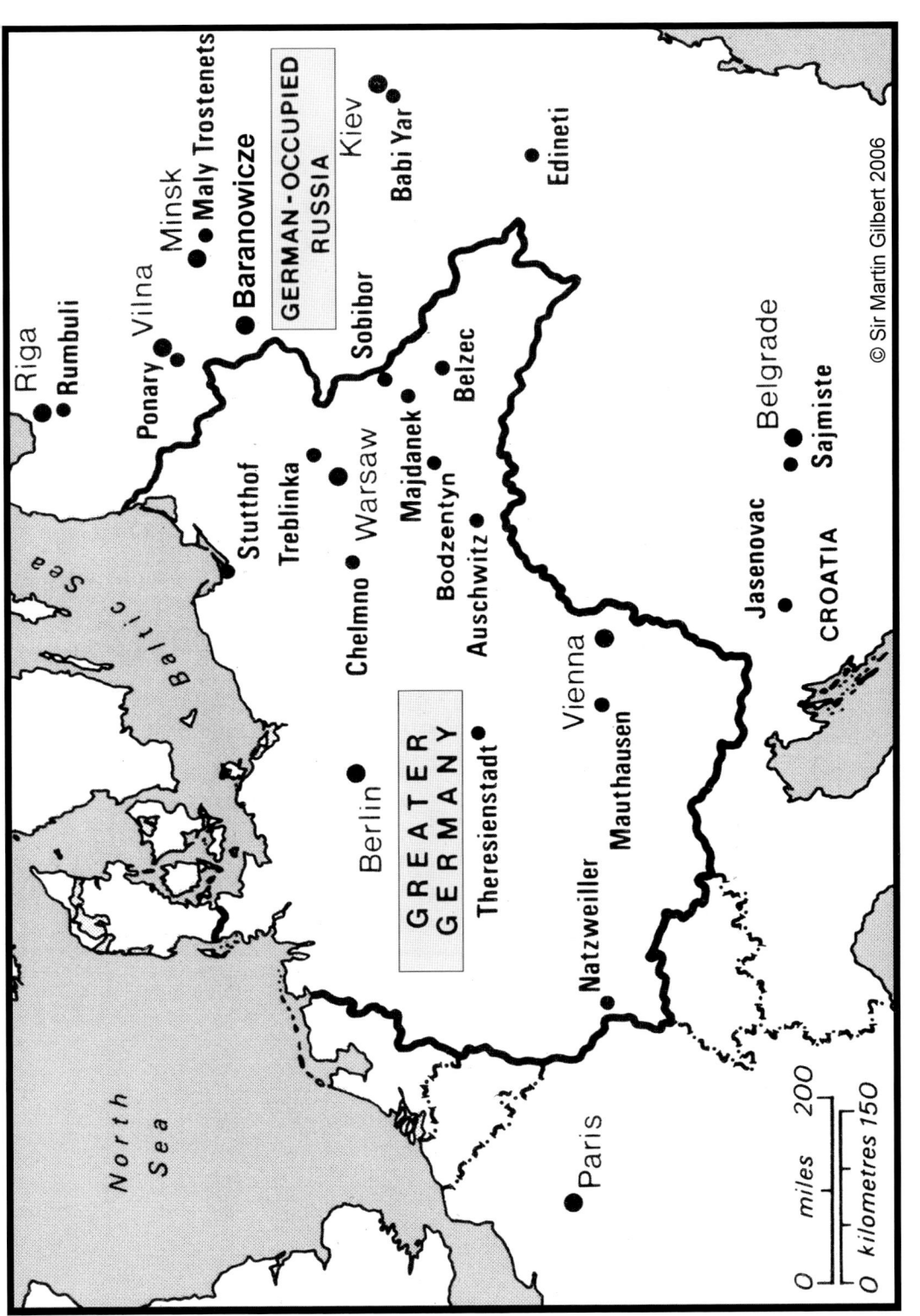

civilized, were suddenly too good for the Jews. It was into the street with us, like the vagrants and the homeless, the unwanted and the unclean; herded like animals.

Then another change in the law: that Jews must wear two more solid yellow Stars of David, "fist-sized" patches with the inscription "Jude"; one on the left side of the chest and one on the right side of the back. The penalty for breaking this law, for breaking *any* of the new German laws, was to be arrested and shot. Killed. Young or old, man or woman, mother or child, it didn't matter, this was the law.

These arbitrary, new laws were as demoralizing as they were sudden. Violence we could understand, bullets we could avoid, bombs we could see the damage from. But who could have anticipated and prepared for such humiliation?

I could see the shame in my father's eyes. I could hear the emotion in my mother's throat.

These petty decrees, these dehumanizing messages, were very painful. Where once people whispered, now they stopped and pointed. Where once people murmured, now they spoke aloud, emboldened by the Germans and their new laws, giving voice to their racism, pettiness and mob mentality.

But even with all these new laws, even with the intimidation and the threats, even with the heavy threat of death hanging thickly in the fetid summer air, at this point, we still walked somewhat freely. *If* we wore our yellow Stars of David in all the right places and *if* we walked in the middle of the street – careful to avoid the sidewalk – we could pass unmolested through our town.

But *our* town it was no longer.

Shortly after these laws were instituted we began to hear that in the smaller towns nearby, the Germans were rounding up Jews for labor. Slave labor: digging bunkers or trenches, repairing roads damaged by heavy military equipment; back-breaking toil in the hot summer sun. There were even rumors that if the Jews resisted, they were swiftly and mercilessly killed. Shot in cold blood, right where they stood.

At first, even with all the evidence, these rumors were scoffed at. After all we were a civilized people. Dignified. Refined. We had surrendered to the Germans, been humbled by their bombs and complied with their arbitrary rules.

But soon we would learn the truth. We would realize that the rumors were all *too* true. The threats of violence would turn brutal, the whispered killings become real. Being forced to dig trenches and fix roads were the least of our worries.

One day I slipped carelessly into a peaceful daydream and out of sheer habit walked on the sidewalk by accident. A German soldier stopped me immediately and screamed in my face, his spittle hot and raw against my ashen cheeks, "Du fafluhte Jude (you dirty Jew), how dare you walk on the sidewalk."

I was terrified. My heart was beating so fast I thought it would explode out of my chest. I thought my legs would buckle from beneath me as my knees shook out of fear and humiliation.

The German soldier continued to scream and curse at me, his breath hot on my pale, ashen face and I could only think that I was going to be killed for something as stupid as walking on the sidewalk in my town, the town that I was born in.

Instead he hit me in the side with the heavy butt of his rifle and then kicked me a few times in my legs as other people on the sidewalk watched in terror. Then, as quickly as my ordeal had started, it was over. That nameless, faceless German soldier left happily, singing as he bragged carelessly, "I beat up a Jew! I beat up a dirty Jew!"

He was superhuman. I was subhuman. My crime? I was a Jew walking on the sidewalk. We Jews were not fit to walk among the living. Marked with yellow Stars of David, we Jews could be shot on sight for our "transgressions."

That soldier had taught me all of those things in a very few tense seconds. Things that I must never forget, not for a moment, for fear of death. I was lucky – blessed, actually – that he did not shoot me where I stood, trembling and sweating beneath his withering brutality.

That was my first contact with the brutality and violence that would become commonplace in the days, weeks and years ahead.

# ROUNDUPS

The Germans started to round up Jewish people for labor: slave labor. One day while I was walking in the street, the Nazis descended upon us and rounded up a few hundred Jewish men, myself included.

We were shouted at, screamed at, grabbed, punched, prodded, kicked, pushed and forced to stand at attention, which we didn't even know how to. We weren't soldiers.

We were old men, young boys, accountants, teachers, butchers, librarians and bakers. More shouting, more kicking, more screaming, until at least we stood up straight, trying to be still, despite trembling hands and shaking knees. The Germans selected 73 men. Just like that, "You, you, you, and you," and took them away before anyone realized what had happened.

The rest of us were sent home. The next day we were told by the gentiles, the non-Jewish residents of Baranowicze, that the German soldiers took the 73 men to the nearby forest to dig ditches. When the men finished the work, the Germans killed them in cold blood.

Shot them, one by one, in the back with machine guns. Then they buried those 73 innocent men – fathers, grandfathers, brothers, nephews, boyfriends and husbands – in the ditches they had just dug with their own bare hands and covered them with the soil they had dug up.

When news of these killings spread through town – this first mass execution, the murder of Jewish men – our innocence was irrevocably lost.

We now understood that the Germans were capable of anything: that soldiers would stand idly by smoking cigarettes and making jokes while Jews dug their own graves a mere few feet away, then kill and bury them. We now knew that monsters like these would stop at nothing.

Of course it was not lost on me that but for the sake of a man next to me – on the left or the right, in front or behind – being chosen instead of me, I would have been lying at the bottom of that heap of bodies instead of in my bed. I slept fitfully that night. Not grateful, not thankful, not even relieved, just numb. It could have been me, I thought, over and over and over again, It could have been me.

A few days later I was walking down another street when I was caught in a similar roundup. This time the Germans had gathered a few hundred men: shouting, kicking, prodding, poking, until finally we were standing in front of them trembling at attention – how quickly we learn – each one of us remembering what had happened to those 73 poor men only days earlier.

This time the crafty Nazi soldiers asked the group who could handle horses. In mere seconds, that was all that it took, 29 men raised their hands and the Germans whisked them away. Just like before, the rest of us went home or to work.

As we feared, as we dreaded, the 29 men never returned.

A few weeks after, we found out that those 29 men had helped to transport stolen Polish horses all the way to Germany. At the end of their long and perilous journey, the German soldiers killed every one of them.

I had a very close friend in that group, Gary Starinski. A young boy my age, he knew how to handle horses. I wondered, What were his last thoughts? What went through his lonely, frightened mind as he faced down the cold, steel barrel of a dirty Nazi rifle? Gary was the first of my dear friends to die at the hands of the Germans.

I always wondered after that experience, that close call, why those 29 men had raised their hands. It seemed foolish to me. Stupid even. Especially knowing what had happened to those first 73. But then I remembered how I felt when the German soldiers first asked, "Which of you can handle horses?" I remembered thinking to myself; maybe if I say I can handle horses, I will be spared. Maybe they are going to kill everyone in this roundup who can't handle horses. Maybe that is their trick. Then I thought, but if I say I can handle horses and really can't, I will surely be killed. I should just keep my hands at my side. I went back and forth like that, over and over. I had only a few seconds to decide. Should I raise my hand? Should I keep it by my side? Will I be killed if I do? Will I be killed if I don't?

You never knew with the Germans. It could have gone either way. Yes or no? Left or right? Raise your hand? Keep it at your side? On this particular day, in this particular roundup, to this particular question, what was the right answer?

You never knew when you would be rounded up, asked a question upon which your life depended and carted away to your death. Live or die– You just never knew.

You didn't have to be present during a roundup to feel the cold hand of death creep across your shoulder, to feel those cold, dead fingers brush past your cheek to take the life of someone else.

Sometimes what I saw from afar was almost as bad as being there; even worse.

Sometimes I just wanted it to go away, no matter what it took.

Sometimes death didn't seem so bad.

---

On another occasion the Germans rounded up about 300 men and women from the quiet streets of Baranowicze. They assembled them, kicking and screaming, in front of a beautiful Catholic Church that had a lovely park on the side and a lush green expanse of manicured lawn at the front with beautiful pine trees. The German soldiers ordered the men to lie face down on the ground.

Some of the men resisted, but after much kicking, prodding and beating, these few resistors gave in.

There on the grass, helpless and defenseless, the soldiers ordered the Jewish men to squeeze close to each other, closer and closer, until they formed a "human floor." Then, on the church's hallowed ground, the German soldiers ordered the shivering young women in the crowd to undress. When they hesitated, when they balked, the Nazis tore at their garments, ripping them to shreds and tossing the women to the human "mat" roughly. Then the German soldiers raped the young women in front of everybody, lying down on top of the men on the ground, their crisp uniform pants now puddled at their ankles. The men below squirmed, hearing the cries of the women on their backs, feeling the soldiers' rough boots between their legs, their faces buried in grass and dirt to hide their tears of shame and anguish.

When the Nazis were through raping our women, when they were spent, they pulled up their trousers and continued the torture. They ordered the women to dance on top of the men, clapping and singing as they danced.

Ravaged and traumatized, it was all the women could do to

force themselves to stand up, naked and horrified. When some of them lost their balance and fell, the German soldiers beat them without mercy.

Somewhere music was playing; soldiers were singing, drinking and having an impromptu party in the middle of the day. And then, suddenly, an extended barrage of machine gun fire replaced the music. The Nazis killed them all. Each and every man and woman.

All of them: the women who had lain under those insane German soldiers, suffering their sodomy, crying, screaming in their hearts; and the men who had betrayed their very souls to stay quiet and still, lest the women be hurt all the more. Naked and beaten, trampled and stomped, they were all killed.

Nearby, a silent testament to the cold and premeditated nature of their vicious attack, trucks waited to take the dead bodies to the forest, where other dead Jews had dug graves shortly before.

That day 300 Jews died, 300 Jewish men and women, 300 neighbors and friends; 300 lives snuffed out.

How do I know? What would make me describe such horrible things? Where did I learn the intimate and disgusting details of this feast of barbarism?

I was there. I watched this incident – horrified, panicked and disgusted – from across the street where I worked. I felt their pain. I watched their tears fall. I saw their naked bodies white and bruised in the midday sun. I heard their screams and the sounds from the machine guns. I saw it all!

I remember wondering what was going on in the minds of those women being raped by the German soldiers in front of their friends, relatives and neighbors. I remember wondering, too, what was going on in the minds of the men beneath them, lying on the ground while their friends, sisters, aunts – even their girlfriends and wives – were being violently raped on their backs!

Should they get up and fight? Defend their women? Should the women resist? Turn away? Kick and bite? Fight back? Would they be killed anyway? Would they be spared? Did they suffer through those brutal attacks, through those vicious rapes, hoping against hope that by submitting to the German soldiers they would somehow save themselves? Did the men hold back as well thinking their anger, violence and resistance would only bring more wrath upon the women writhing on their backs? How do you react when one day you are simply grabbed off the street screaming and savagely raped by crude strangers in stiff green uniforms with wild, angry eyes and vodka-soaked breath covering your screaming mouth? To fight or not to fight?

These thoughts filled my head for days, germinating into a thick, red flower of hatred, violence and revenge. I was sixteen at the time. I knew some of the girls they had raped, some of the women they had killed. The men, too. Most of us knew each other. These were not strangers.

To shoot a man quickly was one thing. To make him lie on the ground then savagely rape a woman on top of him was quite another. It was perverted and twisted.

That day marked the end of all sense of hope.

The bombings had chipped some of it away in Baranowicze. The brief escape attempt to Minsk then back. The firefight with German and Russian bullets whizzing over my head. The German laws had eaten away at my pride and the roundups had drained all hope from the very marrow of my bones. This orgy, this slaughter, this massacre, sucked whatever hope was left and spit it out on the ground to mingle with the soldiers' semen, the women's tears and the blood of the Jews.

I felt we were all dead now.

All of us.

Each and every Jew in Baranowicze.

It was just a matter of time.

# LIVING WITH DEATH

One day I could not go to the Polish military barracks where I was working for the Germans as a carpenter. I was sick and feverish with a sharp rasp on the back of my throat. Sitting under a tree in our backyard for some much-needed fresh air, I began to get bored. I was sick, sure, but young and restless as well.

While I knew the ever-present danger of the occupying German forces was always just a boot stomp away, I found myself letting my guard down somewhat. For some reason, even though I didn't really need to, I decided to use the bathroom before returning to the house for a little nap.

Our bathroom was situated in back of our barn, behind the house. The minute I walked in and closed the door, the very minute that I had latched the door shut, I heard loud screams coming from outside: "Du fafluhte Jude, get out of the houses, you dirty Jews, get out."

I suddenly realized that they were looking for Jewish men. Another roundup. Another selection.

I decided to sit in the toilet and wait it out. I sat there and resolved that in case they came in my direction, before I would allow them to grab me, I would slip quietly into the ditch with the human waste.

It didn't matter to me, it was better than death. That was how far we had come since the Germans invaded Baranowicze. That was how low we had fallen under the Nazi oppression. Better to hide in the filth and refuse than risk my life on the whim of some Nazi soldier. My will to live was bigger, more important than the pride that kept me from jumping into that waste.

Yes, we were Jews. Yes, our town had been occupied by the

vicious Germans. Yes, we had to wear yellow Stars of David on our shoulders and backs and could no longer walk on the sidewalks. Yes, our town had been ravaged by the German bombs and the Nazi oppressors were the new "gods" of our daily lives. But we were still alive. And staying alive mattered. As fearful as we were, as horrible as our situation was, life was still better than the alternative.

"Du fafluhte Jude, get out of the houses, you dirty Jews, get out!" I listened to the soldiers' screams, one leg dangling above the human filth, the other poised on the wooden floor. The seconds ticked by, beads of sweat dropping from my brow.

Any second I expected to hear the crunch of boots on gravel. Any second I expected the door to be kicked open and a pair of rough Nazi hands to reach in and grab me from my hideout. Any second I expected to be discovered, captured and killed.

Then, as suddenly as it had begun, the roundup was over.

The German soldiers picked up some men and left as quickly as they had come. I waited silently; sweat dripping off me, until I was sure they were gone, then went back to the house.

Of course the men who were gathered up, those not lucky enough to have been caught with their pants down in their outhouses, never returned.

Yes, there were worse things than death. This I knew too well by now. Life was precious, indeed, but fear and oppression, slavery and betrayal, rape and shame and the threat of death were in some ways more painful, more agonizing, more deadly than death itself. Still, I felt lucky to be alive.

It was a miracle that I hadn't been inside taking a nap when the Nazis came. A miracle that I had gone outside for fresh air.

A miracle that a trip to the bathroom saved my life.

Other times I was not so lucky. One day while working to repair damaged barracks for the engineering corps of a military outfit, I was taken by truck with another kid, my friend Misha Schinitski, to pick up lumber from the lumberyard. I was sixteen and Misha was seventeen.

We stood in the truck-bed. One soldier went into the office to take care of the paperwork. The driver stayed in the cabin to clean his rifle. When he was finished, he aimed his rifle at a Jewish man walking across the street and, just like that pulled the trigger, killing him instantly. His partner ran out of the office to see what happened. The driver nonchalantly assured him that the he had simply tried out his rifle, not to worry, that nothing had happened. Nothing! Just an unfortunate Jew shot dead on the street.

Another day 80 of us were dragged off the streets and put to work in a nearby military bakery. We already had jobs and might be fired for not showing up on time. We had families at home with no idea where we were, if we were dead or alive.

When the Nazis picked you off the streets, you went with them whenever they said go. Or else.

At the bakery we were forced to carry 100-pound bags filled with flour from trucks to a warehouse about 100 feet away. Back and forth, from the truck to the warehouse, again and again and again.

To overstate the obvious, 100 pounds is heavy. Merely lifting it up off the ground is sheer agony. Hoisting it over your shoulder is a feat of Herculean strength. It is bruising, backbreaking to do over and over, again and again, all day long. I guess this is why it was called slave labor.

The bags were heavy and the work brutal. The sun hot. The day long. My back screamed, my legs cried, the sweat stung my eyes. I faltered, I fell, I got back up. However, the fear of being brutally beaten or even shot to death by German soldiers loitering nearby with smoldering cigarettes and loaded machine guns gave me a strength I never knew that I possessed.

It was my first time forced into slave labor and I learned to survive it as best I could: minute by minute, hour by hour, day by day, 100-pound bag by 100-pound bag. I worked there for one week, and even though I was a strapping, young sixteen year-old boy in peak physical condition, it nearly killed me. There was no pay, of course, and only watery soup for lunch and dinner.

We kept at it ten hours a day, and to make sure that the bakery had the same workers – alive and on time the next morning – they kept us overnight. Battered and exhausted, we slept heavily on the dewy grass under a tree for six straight nights. They pushed us without mercy, worked us relentlessly and sapped our strength until there was none left. We were not men to those soldiers, we were robots, machines and dogs.

We had to forget everything but the weary path we walked from truck to warehouse and back again under the oppressive weight of those deadly bags of flour.

Some of us were beaten viciously for not working fast enough. Like wolves, the German soldiers ferreted out the weak, the nearsighted, the overweight, the lame and bullied them mercilessly, the butts of their rifles as hard and unforgiving as stone.

One man dropped to the ground and died. The German soldiers left him where he was, and worked the rest of us all the harder to make up for the loss of one man. We were lucky: after the week was over, the Germans let us go home.

We survived. Bruised, battered, shamed and humiliated. We survived. We limped home to grateful mothers, crying wives, relieved daughters. We survived. We ate greedily, talked little and slept heavily. We survived. We dried our tears, counted our blessings, hugged our families, savored a cup of hot coffee and prayed and praised from the very bottom of our very grateful hearts. We survived.

We realized how miraculous it was to return home – alive. Others were not so lucky.

---

The Jews of Baranowicze were not the only victims. The Germans also rounded up all the gypsies, about 500 men, women and children, and killed them, too. Then the Germans rounded up all the Jehovah's Witnesses, about 50 of them, and all the cripples and homosexuals, and killed them as well. Whole families wiped out; never again to exist.

In two-and-a-half short months of occupation and repression, the German soldiers killed about 1,500 Jews in roundups in our town of Baranowicze.

The roundups were bad, but they were not the end. They were not as bad as it would get. Another twisted and insane perversion of the natural order devised by the Nazis would be worse: the ghettos. They would be worse.

# Part 3
# The Ghetto

"I HAVE LIVED TO SEE JEWISH DEFENSE IN THE GHETTO IN ALL ITS GREATNESS AND GLORY."

- Mordechai Anielewicz, a martyr of the Warsaw Ghetto Uprising

# THE GHETTO IS ESTABLISHED

*Rosh Hashanah 1941*

On Rosh Hashanah, the Jewish New Year, the German authority established a ghetto in Baranowicze. It was the first of many Jewish – and Christian – holidays to be marred by massive German operations that affected the Jews in life-threatening ways.

This was no accident. The Germans realized how important religion was to our people, to people in general. The Nazis took every opportunity to trample on our beliefs through surprise, fear, violence and degradation.

Nothing was sacred, not even Rosh Hashanah, the "birthday of mankind."

Traditionally Rosh Hashanah is celebrated as the day on which God created Adam, God's final and most precious creation. In Hebrew, Rosh Hashanah means literally "head of the year," or "first of the year."

Traditionally it is a sacred time to begin careful introspection, look back at the mistakes of the past year and plan for the year ahead.

But not in 1941. And for many Jews, never again. For in September 1941, Rosh Hashanah took on an entirely new – and sinister – meaning in my hometown of Baranowicze.

There was to be no prayer, no introspection, no looking back at the mistakes of the past year and certainly no plans for the future. Who knew if there was going to be a tomorrow, a next week, a next month – let alone any *real* future.

Any plans we were foolish enough to make were quickly dashed by the Germans. They dictated what jobs we could work, where we could walk and what we could wear. And now they were telling us where we could live.

We had heard rumors about what the ghetto would be like from other local towns or villages. We had known that a ghetto was forming and had heard the construction, had seen the fences and the shiny glint of barbed wire, and yet, we lived in a numbed state of denial.

Who could blame us, really? The fear of daily roundups and the threat of instant death hung like a gray and sticky fog over our daily lives. How could we imagine, how could we foresee the reality of what was to come? How could we have eaten, how could we have slept, how could we have *lived* if we had fully realized how bad it would *actually* get?

For weeks while we toiled away at slave labor, the Germans had been erecting a fence around one small corner of our beautiful town. Rose gardens gave way to ditches, shrubs were ripped out and fence posts driven in. About twenty square blocks were emptied to prepare the ghetto, and the barbed wire began on *our* side of the street so that German soldiers could keep watch over their captives: the Jews.

Where once had been trees, shrubs, flower beds and pansies, now stood a barrier. Ugly and dull, powerful and brutal, the fence took on a life of its own. It grew higher and higher, finally standing 7 feet. Seven solid feet of shiny, razor-sharp barbed wire put an end to all thoughts of escape, and that was even before we were crammed inside.

The word "ghetto" was rarely used.

The Germans called it "the Jewish section" of Baranowicze, a milder misnomer. We took up this name as well. It was neater and cleaner to think that we would soon be moving to the Jewish section of town; a neighborhood where we could all be together, working for the common good, struggling to survive among our own.

On the evening before Rosh Hashanah, as we were respectfully preparing for our sacred holiday, word spread that we would be moving to the ghetto the next morning. Posters bearing written notices were plastered in the center of town and all along the light posts lining the sidewalks where we could no longer walk. As the Nazis advanced through our streets, passing the doors of the gentiles and banging only on those of the Jews, neighbors, friends and families kept each other abreast of the latest developments.

As my parents shook their heads, as my brother and I cowered, we learned that the rumors were true. Finally as my father and I returned home from another day of forced labor, we saw the notices for ourselves and rushed to join our family.

It had happened: the Jewish section of town, the ghetto, had opened.

We had twenty-four hours to move. One day. We could not use a horse and buggy, a wagon or a coach. Whatever we could fit on our backs, whatever we could haul at our sides, we were allowed to bring. Nothing more. Most of our furniture, our heirlooms, our priceless family pictures, we had to leave behind. We were given an address and ordered to report there the next day. That was it. Life as we knew it, brutal as it was, was over.

Goodbye old house.

Goodbye barn in the backyard.

Goodbye freedom.

My father shrewdly spent most of the evening planning how best to move as much as possible, while my mother used her own considerable skills to find unique ways of filling every pant pocket or handkerchief with precious heirlooms, antiques or pieces of silver.

We slept fitfully the last night in our family home and woke early the next morning to begin the dreaded move to the ghetto.

We wore three pairs of pants and seven shirts! We walked

like zombies, a pack filled with silverware or dishes strapped to each of our backs. My father lugged a trunk, my mother two suitcases.

Back and forth we went, past the grocer's, past the theater, past the gentiles nodding smugly, to the Jewish section, then past the barbed wire fence, through the imposing front gate and into the unfamiliar streets of a strange neighborhood.

We were not alone in our new quarters. Our new home was filled with almost 50 other Jewish people – families, couples and strangers. Other families mingled, more and more of them arriving by the hour, dropping off their own possessions in shifts, as we returned to our house yet again for more goods, more food and more clothes.

By the evening we had managed to smuggle as much as possible into our own living space and my father saw that we could fit no more. The Germans had given each Jew in the ghetto one square yard of space in which to live, eat, sleep and breathe. Hardly enough room to stand up spread out your arms and turn around in. Yet this was where we were to spend the rest of the German occupation. For a family of four, like ours, this meant four square yards for our whole family – one square yard each.

Nervously we introduced ourselves to the other occupants, who were just as scared and nervous as we were. We milled around the house, finding our way, stumbling around unfamiliar corners, separating our cupboards for food storage, filling the closets.

The Germans had moved all the gentiles out of the homes, cottages, barns and lofts that made up the ghetto. Only one family used to live in our new house. We saw the remnants of their lives left behind and abandoned everywhere we turned: an old hairbrush, a half-filled packing crate in the corner, yellow squares on the walls where family pictures once hung.

My father's accountant brain quickly did the math: about 10

families were assigned to "our" new house. That meant the gentiles who had given up their family home had ten other houses to choose from on the other side of town; the clean side, now *"Juden Rein"* (free of Jews).

I imagined some other family rifling through the things we had to leave behind. Roughly handling the clock that was too heavy for my father to carry all the way across town. Kicking at the family couch, our couch, to see if it was sturdy enough for them. Turning up their noses at the dust left behind from such a hasty move: old broken toys, dirty dishes, curtains still hanging from a crooked rod; framed portraits of our relatives, strangers to them but beloved to us.

That night, before we went to bed, my father prayed and my mother cried. All the Jews of Baranowicze cried.

The naïve hope that we had felt at the thought of living in a Jewish section started to fade as the fall of 1941 turned into winter.

My father and I were still able to work outside the ghetto, but now we had to pass through the single front gate each morning and return through its imposing archway every evening. Twice daily. It was a silent but grim reminder that our freedom was a thing of the past. Inside, too, the lack of freedom surrounded us.

First they enforced a curfew. From 8 p.m. until 6 a.m. no Jew in the ghetto was allowed outdoors. It gave those of us who worked just enough time to get home from a long day at the factory or the plant or, in our case, the nearby airfield, where we fixed roads and restored burned down buildings. It gave the women and the elderly just enough time to shop in a hastily setup market for stale bread and sour tomatoes.

The curfew was bad and affected us in many unexpected ways. For instance, our new home did not have indoor plumbing. Outhouses served us instead and we could only use those during the day when we were "free." But in the evening, after curfew, going outside after dark could result in death. German soldiers patrolled the perimeter looking for any opportunity to begin – or end – their shift with a dead Jew who had sneaked out to relieve himself.

Instead the German soldiers gave us a pail for our human waste. One pail per room. It sat in the middle of the room, another symbol of German occupation and Jewish degradation. We all had to use it. All 50 of us in the house. After eight in the evening until six in the morning, once curfew had gone into effect, we had to relieve ourselves in front of everybody.

In the beginning this was almost impossible. Especially for the women. I remember my mother crying the first time she saw "the pail." But even for the men, it was degrading and embarrassing. I still remember the first time I used the pail. It makes me blush to this day. I was sixteen at the time and there were other youngsters in the house with us, including young girls.

But what could we do? When we had to go, we went. After a while, like so many of the morbid details in our daily lives, we got used to it. It is amazing what human beings can adapt to under the threat of death. Still others felt so shocked, so embarrassed and so degraded that they risked life and limb to use the nearby outhouses after curfew. Just next door to us, a neighbor tried using the bathroom behind his barn after curfew and was shot and killed on sight.

Still, there are some things worse than death.

The smell from "the pail" became overbearing; unbearable. It permeated the wooden beams, the furniture, the drapes, even our clothes. It was everywhere, all the time. Fifty people – men and women, young and old, sick and well, all using the same pail for nearly twelve hours every night.

I dreaded entering the house for the stench of it. Still, we persevered. We had to. We had no choice.

There were other struggles as well. The rations of food were one hundred grams of bread a day, one pound of potatoes and one half a pound of flour per week. No milk. No salt. No sugar. Hunger became a burden too.

My father did manage to find one way to improve our cramped living conditions. At the site where he worked, he bartered for lumber, and every day he would bring home a new two by four or four by four. In this way he was slowly able to assemble a three-story bunk bed for our family. On the bottom bunk, he slept with my mother, above him was my little brother, and high above them all, on the top, was where I slept.

The beds were not big; barely enough for one person, but stacking them allowed us more space, more breathing room at floor level. In this way, working each day, avoiding roundups with our work permits and building bunk beds, we were able to fool ourselves into thinking that we were living a "normal" life.

And, in a way, compared to what would happen later, we were. Because at this point the ghetto was not sealed. Yes, there was barbed wire, a curfew and a gate. Yes, there were guards on the perimeters and the occasional crackle of gunfire. But the gate was open and the guards only appeared at night. So we could sneak in toiletries without the fear of getting shot, or bread from lunch at work, or lumber and nails for something as simple as a bunk bed.

While we were free to walk through the front gate, we still had to wear the yellow star on our clothes and walk in the middle of the street. We were also able to walk to and from work without guards. We could even visit people we knew from before the war.

However not too many of our old gentile "friends" wanted to see us anymore. And even if they did, even if the odd gentile shopkeeper or librarian passing on the street wanted to say hello, it was awkward and unpleasant. Here we were reeking of "the pail" and marked for death, the yellow stars on our shoulders burning like hot pokers as we stood in the middle of the street talking to the gentiles standing on the sidewalk.

Like a blood-red stain, the German poison seeped into every corner of "free" Baranowicze. We found ourselves returning to the ghetto sooner and sooner. We weren't welcome anywhere else, that was clear. The Nazi hatred permeated the entire town in the same way that "the pail" stank up our whole house.

How low we had fallen since the Germans invaded in June! August found us cringing at new laws, September found us huddled into four by five blocks of living space, packed like sardines in a can, oily and smelly, literally forcing the gentiles to turn up their noses.

We walked like condemned men, shunned, hated and feared. We knew it was all part of the Nazi plan. We knew that in each occupied town all across Poland or Belarus the same process was applied.

First the Germans crushed our Russian protectors, sending them scurrying into the forests. Next came the edicts, the new laws and then the roundups. They were smart in their calculated brutality: don't shock them right away, lull them into submission.

The randomness of violence, the constant state of shock. Kill a few Jews, then kill some more. Build a ghetto, but don't call it a ghetto, call it a "section," a Jewish section. Erect a wall, throw up a fence, build a gate and round them up. Move the gentiles out, promise them new houses (confiscated Jewish houses). Cram the Jews into houses, six, eight, ten families to a dwelling. Give them a curfew. Make them relieve themselves in pails. Degrade them. Humiliate them. But let them live. Starve them slowly. Work them hard. All the while whispering to the gentiles: "See how dirty the Jews are, see how pale, how unhealthy, how scared. They are not like us. They are not like *you*. We are better than you, but you are still better than them. Ignore them on the streets. They are not your friends. They never were. They are your enemies."

And it worked. It worked like clockwork. Over and over again. In Polish towns near and far, the Jews succumbed to this efficiently brutal pattern of events. We shrugged, lucky to be alive. Fortunate to feel hungry, happy to piss in pails. We thanked God we were still around for one more day, hoping the allies would soon come to our rescue and save us.

Then we could rip off our stars, walk on the sidewalks, use the outhouses, strut after dark, quit crying in our sleep and wake without wondering would today be the day?

But no Russians returned. No allies came.

We were alone in Baranowicze. Strangers in our own town.

And the roundups continued.

In October 1941 German soldiers grabbed me and my father in a roundup of about 1,000 men, assembling us by the little park in the open field next to the city theater. There was no raising of hands this time. The men selected for work were carted away in trucks. I was sixteen and really scared. I did not want to die. I was not ready. I had learned from previous roundups that most of the time men selected for slave labor never returned. They were killed by the German soldiers after the work was done.

My father tried to comfort me and told me that somehow things would work out. It did not help. I did not stop shivering – how could I when all around me I saw grown men crying and calling on God to save them. I was afraid, but I did not cry. Finally, when he came to me, the German soldier told me to leave the park and go back to work. My father and I were holding onto each other, comforting each other and the German just let us both leave. We found out the next day that about 350 men had been picked and forced to build a camp to house the Russian soldiers, now prisoners of war. Next the men dug trenches around the camp the size of two football fields and installed barbed wire fences around the entire perimeter. After they had finished the German soldiers killed them all, burying them in the trenches they had just dug.

The Germans brought about 100,000 Russian POWs into that camp, which had no facilities of any kind. No toilets, no running water, no mess tent, no ovens, no stoves, nothing but a cold patch of ground with barbed wire fence around it. That and a trench bearing the rotting bodies of 350 Jews. The Russian POWs slept on the ground huddled together to keep warm.

Over the next few months most of those POWs died of starvation, sickness or the freezing cold of the severe November weather. Nobody was allowed to give them food or supplies. Luckily a few thousand of them managed to escape into the dense forests nearby. At the time I simply thought, Good for them. They escaped the German killers. Maybe one day, they would come back with reinforcements and kill them all!

Little did I know, that those few thousand Russian soldiers who escaped, would be the beginning, the first of the Russian partisan movement – the Russian underground.

# GHETTO IS SEALED

*Christmas 1941*

My father, my mother, my brother and I began the winter of 1941 in the ghetto.

By then we had gotten used to the way things worked. The curfew was bad, the space was cramped, the pail was still agony, but we were alive. We could walk through the gate in the morning, lucky to go to this job or that job, swinging our lunch pails in the morning air and be free of the ghetto for eight hours.

We could feel the sun on our faces, breathe in fresh air to alleviate the stench from our house and be relatively free.

September faded, October and November blurred together into frosty days and nights, then December dawned bright and cold and the weather worsened.

So did our tenuous hold on life.

It started on December 18, 1941, the week of Christmas. The Germans perversely seemed to enjoy wreaking havoc during the holiday seasons. As families gathered and prayer books emerged, the Nazis sealed the ghetto, intruding on the sanctity of Jews worship; it had been speculated for days. After all, you didn't put up a 7-foot, barbed wire fence, then leave the gate open all day. You didn't leave the gate open and then enforce a curfew all night. You didn't have guards just at night unless you were preparing to have them during the day. You didn't build a doghouse just for looks.

The week of the holiday, more guards appeared. Not just at the front gate where there were always five or six glaring silently as you ambled past, but along the four sides of that big barbed wire fence as well.

One guard started at his corner and the second started at the opposite end of the fence. They walked toward each other, marching in precision – their steely eyes peeled for "subversive" Jewish behavior – and when the two met in the middle, they turned around and headed back. It went on like that, day after day, twenty-four hours a day.

Now to go to work we had to be escorted by German soldiers. They lined us up in a column – pushing, prodding, shoving, poking, hitting and punching – and forced us to walk in rows, almost marching military style. They held their machine guns at the ready to shoot us down on the slightest pretext.

You may wonder why I always tried to get a job. The answer: survival.

When we worked for the Germans, we were given a piece of paper, a work permit, allowing us to be out on the streets in case a soldier stopped you.

Many times the Germans stopped us anyway. They would split us into two lines: those with working papers and those without. Often, those without work permits never returned home. So the piece of paper we got on each job was often the difference between life and death. For this piece of paper, my father and I would have worked twenty-four hours a day, seven days a week.

Many times, it felt that that's what we did.

My father was an excellent worker, dedicated and brilliant, and shortly after we moved to the ghetto he found a steady job in a nearby army base that was part of an engineering division, a regiment that took care of German cars and trucks. At this factory they repaired and restored the vehicles that had been damaged during the *blitzkrieg*.

It was a big factory and my father's job was to manage the laundry. That laundry had 30 Jewish girls working there, washing everything by hand. From his first day on the job my father felt as if he had gained thirty daughters. He was a man who couldn't help feeling protective of people, and I knew exactly what that meant.

To keep an eye on me, to protect me, my father always tried to have us work together. My father found a job for me in that same company. We were lucky to work together in one place. The fear of death was in our thoughts constantly. Night and day, my father wore a grim look from the constant worry about his family. I realized then that working with my father was a precious gift.

The company was named H.K.P. Optailung. My job was to repair or copy the broken parts of various German trucks and automobiles. Because I was artistically inclined I became a special order mechanic and made parts by hand. The Germans liked my work. Sometimes they gave me leftover soup, a cigarette or even a piece of candy for making or repairing a special part for their car.

We couldn't take anything out of the ghetto and we couldn't bring anything into the ghetto. Smuggling food or other necessary items like medicine or soap was punishable by death. This happened quite frequently in the first few weeks after the ghetto was sealed. People didn't understand, didn't *believe,* or they forgot or got lazy. If the Germans caught a Jew with cigarettes in their pockets, or an apple from lunch in their coat, they would take him away. He would be shot or hanged for all to see.

Many mornings we awoke to the sight of Jews hanging in the ghetto square or market. Many were friends, neighbors or, worse, family. Young and old, women and men. There was something eerily hypnotic about their hanging bodies, their necks jerked out of shape, their legs dangling stiff, the squeak of the rope as it moved slowly in the wind. The message was clear: disobey under penalty of death.

Their crimes? Petty, at best. Smuggling in food, being caught after curfew.

Just being a Jew.

They were caught and executed without rules or recourse. Often an overzealous Nazi soldier, no more than eighteen or nineteen years old, was their judge, jury and executioner. Many men, women and children died at the hands of teenagers barely out of puberty.

Gradually the ghetto's Jewish population rose to over 11,500 people, which was more than twice as many Jews as had originally lived in Baranowicze. The Germans had rounded up Jews from nearby villages and put them in the ghetto with us. They even added a few more blocks for the overflow, cramming them in until life became suffocating. Twenty some blocks overflowing with scared, nervous people. We lived like animals. We became animals.

Stuffing us like sardines into houses reeking of human waste, guarding us day and night, working and starving us to death, raping, shooting and hanging us wasn't enough. The Nazis found other ways to satiate their hunger for atrocity.

In the earliest stages of forming the ghetto, the Nazis established a *Judenrat*, or Jewish committee. This committee was made up of Jews of former "position and authority." Rabbis, elders, lawyers, physicians and professionals. We all knew it was an empty post, but still the *Judenrat* did its best to establish law and order inside the ghetto.

The *Judenrat* established local Jewish police to keep order inside the gate. They were not German sympathizers, of course, but merely security guards trying to remind us "to get home before curfew" or "wear your stars."

However neither the *Judenrat* nor their special police force was immune to the heavy hand of the Nazis. After all, they were still Jews. They could be arrested, beat up or shot just like anybody else.

The *Judenrat* were being used by the Germans, we all knew that. They had an office with no locks, authority with no strength and position with no power. All the demands from the German authority went through the *Judenrat*. It was simpler this way.

Shortly after the ghetto was sealed during that bleak and frigid Christmas holiday, the Germans rounded up 100 Jewish men, women and children. This was like no other roundup. There were no lines for the living and the dead. There were no questions: – Who can handle horses? Who is good with their hands? Who has a degree from a university? – There were no choices for these unlucky souls. They were merely hostages, pawns in a Nazi game based on greed.

The Nazis demanded that the *Judenrat* find 100 pounds of gold and 400 pounds of silver inside the ghetto and deliver it to the German authority by noon the next day. The *Judenrat* was shocked. Its president told the German soldiers it was impossible to deliver such a large amount of precious metals in such a short time. The Germans had a quick answer, "Take your police, they suggested, and start pulling gold teeth from your Jews. This is your problem, not ours."

When the ghetto "police" came to us that evening asking for gold and silver, my father explained to them that we had no more gold, it had been bartered a long time ago for food, but that we still had some silver and to come back for it a little later. My mother, my little brother and I cried. This was our precious Passover silver! My mother cherished it. It was a very important heirloom. My great-grandmother had handed it down to my grandmother, who had given it to my mother as a wedding gift. The silver had a long and sentimental family history. It was our treasure. But what could we do? We had to help save 100 Jewish men, women and children. My father packed it and had it ready for the "Jewish police." My mother said a prayer, stopped crying and we all waited in silence for them to pick it up.

During twenty-four tense hours of search and seizure, panic and hysteria, the *Judenrat* and their special police force somehow managed to collect the entire amount of silver, but not the requisitioned amount of gold. They returned to the Nazis begging for mercy. Instead the 100 hostages were taken to prepared graves, lined up and gunned down.

Naturally the Germans kept the silver and the gold.

My family and I had assumed – wrongly – that it could get no worse, that the earlier roundups, before we were moved to the ghetto, were meant to make us think that the ghetto would not be so bad.

We thought the cramped, unlivable conditions, the bone-crushing labor, the starvation diet and the curfews were to be our punishment for the rest of the war.

But the Germans were not done with us Jews.

# LIFE IN THE GHETTO

In January there was a new change in the law. The Nazis decided that we Jews had too much freedom, too much time between getting home from work and the nightly curfew. So they changed the curfew to one hour earlier, 7 p.m. instead of 8. You couldn't be on the street after the curfew, and since work lasted from sunup to sundown, the moment you returned home, almost to the minute, curfew began.

And the roundups continued, increasing in ferocity, violence and perversion. We feared the end was coming.

No longer did the Germans wait for us to leave our houses before rounding us up in the streets. Now they broke our windows and kicked down our doors. They gave no reasons. They felt like beating you, they beat you. They felt like shooting you, they shot you. Before, there had been some reason to their madness – stealing horses, digging mass graves, repairing a road, building a POW camp – now they simply rounded you up.

They beat you up before work, spit at you, cursed at you for not walking fast enough, and punched you for walking too fast. They did the same on the way home. Fresh soldiers meant fresh fear and age didn't matter. To prove they weren't so innocent, a young soldier might kill you *for* blinking twice. To prove he wasn't too old to do the same, an older soldier might kill you for *not* blinking twice.

# THE BARANOWICZE GHETTO

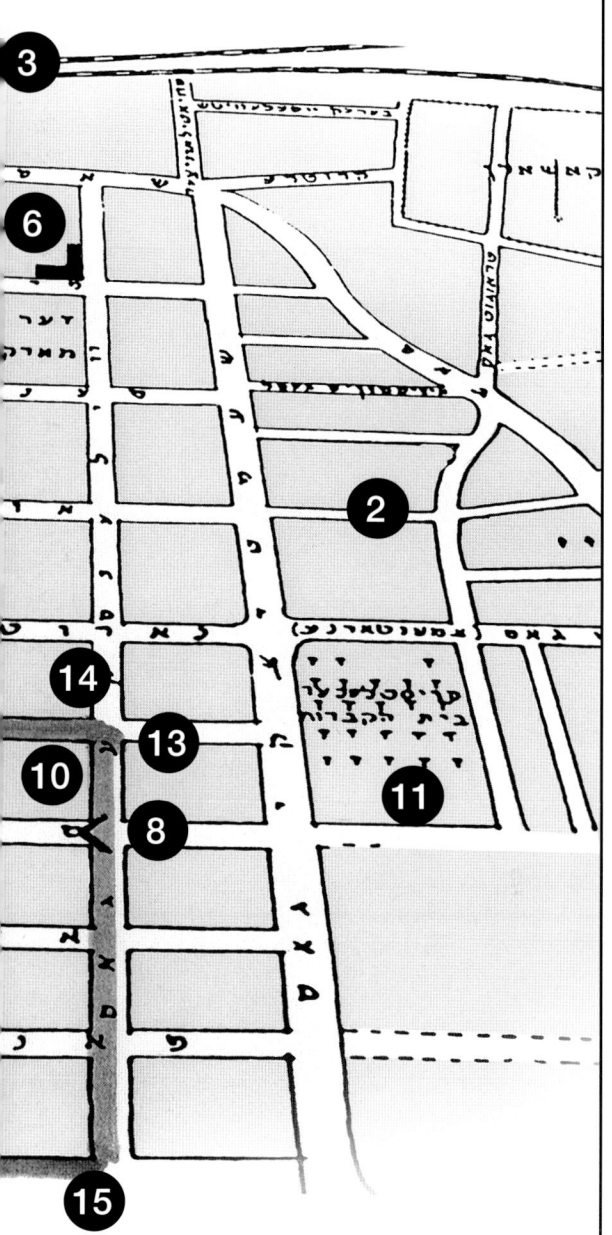

## LEGEND

1. Old town
2. New town
3. Railroad line – Paris to Moscow
4. Baranowicze railway station
5. Old Jewish cemetery
6. Lato home before Nazi occupation
7. Lato living quarters inside ghetto
8. Main entrance to ghetto
9. Rear entrance to ghetto
10. Judenrot – Jewish community center
11. Catholic church – Rape and murder orgy
12. Market- 1st Slaughter – selection for murder
13. Trades Building
14. Electric pole – where policeman was going to kill Samuel
15. Ghetto escape – fence section

Life in the bleak Baranowicze ghetto had been reduced to the smallest of basic pleasures: That first breath of fresh air in the morning *after* the long night with "the pail" and the last breath at night *before* another long night with "the pail"; those final, few golden moments before curfew and the first day of food rations, when we all ate a little too much to compensate for the hunger of the past week.

One day at work, after having lunch with my father and some of the other workers, I took out a cigarette and lit it up like everyone else. I took one puff, grinned, exhaled then took another. My father did not approve of me smoking and looked at me sternly in the way that only he could. He asked me to stop puffing, but I did not. Despite his request and the grim look on his face, I kept on puffing.

It was not like me to disobey my father. When he asked me why I didn't mind him, why I wasn't putting the cigarette out immediately, I said "I did not have much time to enjoy my young life. That everyone knew the Germans were going to kill us, exterminate all the Jews and that I knew that I was going to die young. Maybe today. Maybe tomorrow."

"Please," I begged him, the short lesson becoming very quickly about much more than smoking a cigarette, "let me enjoy what is left of my life."

My father looked at me in silence, crushed. He never said another word, but I saw a tear in his eye that day. From then on he never commented when he saw me smoking. I still remember the expression on his face when I told him that I knew I didn't have much time left to live.

Here was my father, a proud, educated man toiling away at menial labor trying to make the best of it for his family; making the best of circumstances. There was no school that taught how to survive a war. There was no manual on how to live inside a ghetto. There was no guidebook for how to look your wife and children in the eye as you listened to a housemate piss into a pail of human waste in the middle of the night.

With no gun, no weapons, no power at all against the mighty German army, my father did his best, day after day, trying to protect his wife and his two children.

He was a good man, a simple man caught like the rest of us in extraordinary dangerous and deadly circumstances. He knew that his son had lost his childhood forever and it caused him great grief. It even brought him to tears.

If I had not been already dead inside, I might have cried myself.

---

Many Jews continued to deny the undeniable and accept the unacceptable. Despite daily hangings, bloodshed and brutality, the majority of Jews maintained that we should continue exercising caution and obedience. They believed that not making any waves, that bowing and scraping to the German soldiers, was still the best way to avoid death.

Our *Judenrat*, our ruling body inside the ghetto, suggested that any kind of resistance against the Germans would bring down disaster on all Jewish people in the ghetto. My own family and their friends believed this.

I understood their feelings. I respected them. They had responsibilities for other people; they had to worry about the consequences of their actions. I was a teenager, just sixteen years old, and secretly I disagreed with the *Judenrat*, my family and even my own father.

My gut told me that they were wrong. That not all Jews felt this way. That some Jews were ready to fight, no matter what the cost. God knows I never blamed my father for not fighting back, nor my uncles, nor the fathers and uncles of my friends and cousins. They were protecting us in ways we couldn't even fathom, shielding the eyes of their children as they walked by the victims of last night's hanging, steering them from the last roundup, offering up the last crumbs of bread from their empty plates for their children's starving mouths.

No, these brave and fearless Jewish men had enough on their minds.

But my friends and I had heard that some younger Jewish men were starting to organize. That they were meeting, planning and plotting. We heard that a resistance group was forming, or that it already had.

As the clock ticked and our pre-curfew get-togethers drew to a hasty close each night, my friends and I fervently hoped that these rumors might be true. The hope of a resistance movement, the chance to fight back against our German oppressors was one of the few remaining dreams that kept me alive that harsh, cold, brutal ghetto winter.

January drew to a close and despite the frigid temperatures, my father and I trudged off to work every morning always worried that my mother and brother would not be there when we returned later that night, and we were always relieved when, in fact, they greeted us at the door.

At the time I was in the prime of my youth. You would have thought a young boy, his juices flowing, would get excited at the thought of seeing so many women in private moments, so much naked flesh. I say this with utmost truth: I honestly never gave it a single moment's thought.

We were equals in that cramped, crowded house. Jews trying to survive. Young, old, men, women, ugly, pretty – it didn't matter. The fear of death was everywhere, all around us, all the time. Impure thoughts and childish fantasies about the opposite sex had no place in that brutal wasteland of barbed wire and rot.

Though we had grown used to the living room pail, its fetid odor and bilious contents gave off something much worse than odor: bacteria, germs, disease and death. The Germans had killed off most of the Jewish doctors in the ghetto. There was almost no place to find medicine, nowhere to turn for even the slightest medical relief and many Jews began to die from starvation, fever and disease.

Somehow we survived.

I learned to help anyway that I could. Death might be knocking on our doorstep, but in the meantime we needed more food if we were to stay alive. I had always been a creative kid, good with my hands and able to take pieces and parts and create something beautiful from them.

Before the war, before the death, before the ghetto, I had made a pair of ice skates. How foolish they would have been inside the ghetto, how useless, how foreign. Now the stakes were much higher, of course, but I could still use my hands. I could still put my talent to good use to help my family survive.

So I started to make cigarette lighters by hand. Two or three a week, in the beginning. Once I got better, perhaps a new cigarette lighter every day. I would smuggle them into the ghetto, hiding them between my legs where the soldiers didn't check or perhaps in the heel of my boots. I knew I faced certain death if I was caught, but I did it. Proudly. Gladly. Daily.

I had all the tools to make the lighters at the factory where my father and I worked. The German foreman tolerated me because I was a good worker and he didn't want to lose me. I was just a kid. I think he realized that I had the imagination to create something out of nothing. Among the murder and mayhem, among the shame and abuse, I was always surprised when a German showed me any sign of kindness.

Like this foreman who tolerated my sneaky ways and allowed me to go on making lighters in my spare time. I used to sell a cigarette lighter on the black market for a pound of meat. This was a great help to my family. I like to think it allowed us to survive.

My father found a barrel filled with fat. Remembering the recipe from his days as an accountant at a soap factory, he began to make crude bars of soap. Like my cigarette lighters or a hundred other items Jews used to barter with, he traded the soap on the black market for food and other supplies. Extra flour or salt to help my mother stretch our unappetizing meals; medicine, if my brother got sick.

In this way, we were able to scrape by. We were lucky to get through that first harsh winter.

That's how we resisted the Nazis: we survived. Every day we survived was like spitting in their faces. We went on. One day at a time.

In the evenings just before curfew, when my friends and I met, we reminisced about the good times we had had before the war: the good food, the fresh fruits, the candy, the freedom, the sunshine, the rain, the seasons and the holidays. Even school, the homework and the drudgery, all the long hours would have been heaven to us now. Anything but the ghetto. Anything but the war.

We talked of distant forests where we had once gone to pick blueberries, raspberries and mushrooms. We smiled quick shy smiles, suddenly children again. Remembering those sweet smelling meadows, the rivers where we used to go swimming and diving, we wondered how things would be after the war. If we made it. If we lived that long.

Sometimes, lying on my bunk, I would close my eyes and imagine waking up one morning to find that the war was over and there were no more Germans in Baranowicze. No more Nazis, no more gates, no more barbed wire. I don't think that I was the only Jewish person in the ghetto with these dreams, for they were the dreams of thousands of oppressed Jews throughout the ghettos.

Like all nightmares, the reality came back each morning as we awoke to the same crowded bunks, the same reeking pail, the same cramped quarters, the same guards, the same gates and the same barbed wire fences. Our life was a living nightmare from which we could never seem to wake up.

Rumors began to circulate about massive slaughters – deadly massacres – the victims numbering well into the thousands. One day a man came into the ghetto and told the *Judenrat* that in his town the Germans had murdered all of the Jews. It had taken them 5 hours to kill over 2,000 Jews.

Naturally the *Judenrat* did not believe this stranger. They said that he was out of his mind, deranged, crazy, trying to spread fear among the Jews, trying to incite violence against the Germans. Didn't we have enough to worry about? Weren't our lives as horrible as they could possibly get without scaring the women and children even more? So this first man was ignored.

Then, not long after this first man, someone else came into the ghetto with a similar story. Another slaughter. Another massacre. Over 1,000 Jews exterminated, eliminated in just a few hours of cold, calculated Nazi efficiency. The *Judenrat* did not believe this person either. More accusations, more questions, more denial.

Then another man came to the ghetto and said that in his town the Germans had killed 1,500 people in just a few hours.

This time, despite the *Judenrat's* protestations, we Jews in the ghetto finally realized that this *was* true. It was really happening. This was the ugly truth. Like those laws we never thought they'd enact, like the roundups we never thought would happen, like the ghetto that never would be, this time the man's stories sank in and took hold of our daily lives.

We began to believe that this was to be our fate as well, that a slaughter was just around the corner, that it could indeed happen in our town.

But what could we do? Before the ghetto maybe we could have escaped to the forests, run from the streets and hid in the fields. Now we were trapped like rats in a maze. Helpless to defend ourselves, unarmed to fight back, ill-equipped to resist. Our only option was to wait.

Day after day refugees from other villages and nearby ghettos continued to pour into Baranowicze with more stories of slaughter, of mayhem, of carnage, of horror and of death. On top of that our own people began to fear that we would have our own slaughter, our own massacre.

We had made it this far. We had survived so long against such incredible odds, and now what little hope we had was slowly draining. Life became desperate and meaningless, lonely and savage, bitter and cruel.

Death became our constant companion. Every night before we went to sleep, we prayed for life. Every day when we woke up, we dreaded death. It was hopeless, naïve and foolish to think that we would survive. Each sunrise, each new dawn, we believed that we would die. Every night we pinched ourselves to prove we were still alive and we prayed they would not slaughter us while we slept.

It was no life at all. It was a living death.

They had already killed us.

We were already dead.

# THE FIRST SLAUGHTER

*Purim, 1942*

The rumors we had lived with were coming true. At six in the evening on March 2, 1942, just before curfew, the German soldiers sealed the ghetto up tight. Nobody could come in and, more important, nobody could go out.

It was not very difficult to do. By sealing the front gate, they effectively closed off our one and only avenue of escape. Next the Germans split the ghetto in two halves. They rounded up one side and shoved all those Jews into the other side. Half of the ghetto was completely empty and half inundated with twice as many nervous, panic-stricken Jews.

Next the Germans began distributing identification cards. The old, the sick and the lame received green cards. The rest of us received blue cards. We had no way of knowing what these cards were for, what they meant, how they would be used or which card was the "good" color to have. We took them hoping that they meant "life."

Soon we learned that the blue cards signified at least a temporary salvation. The Germans still needed healthy Jews, robust young men and women to build their bridges, repair their roads, dig their trenches and fix their cars. Those of us with blue cards, which fortunately included my whole family, were herded back into the empty part of the ghetto as if it were a version of live checkers.

For a while everything quieted down. The madness of the evening – the screaming, the crying, the praying, the hysteria and the wailing – suddenly stopped. It became quiet. Too quiet. We were more *suspicious* than surprised. Over the last few months we had come to expect the cold calculation and cunning premeditation of the ruthless German Wermacht. My parents did not believe that we were in the clear, nor did I. That night we slept in our clothes, just in case.

The next day was my little brother Jackob's ninth birthday. It was also the Jewish holiday of Purim, the most festive of Jewish holidays, a time of prizes, noisemakers, costumes and treats. But the only prizes we would get on this Purim were bruises from the butts of German rifles. Our noisemakers were the soldiers' cries and harsh screams as they spilled into our homes like a tide of human waste. Our treat – if we were lucky, if we were blessed – was the *gift* of our lives.

At six in the morning of Jackob's birthday German soldiers and Latvian volunteers woke us violently. They broke all the windows with their rifle butts and kicked in all the doors with their boots, screaming, "You dirty Jews, get out of bed, get out of the house!"

Before sunrise they had assembled all of us at the market square across from the public bath.

The first slaughter had begun.

"We're finally going to kill you all," they screamed. We believed them, standing there shaking in the cold morning air, thankful we were wearing our clothes, while other families shivered in their pajamas, robes and slippers.

We were separated into four lines. At the head of each line, an elegantly dressed German civilian was playing god. Ceremoniously, the "god" of our line with one yellow glove on, one yellow glove off, poking out his fist pointing his bare finger to the left and then to the right. Then flicking it to the right again, then to the left. Over and over.

No one knew which side of the line would live or which side would die. Or if all four of the lines would be executed. Or just two or perhaps three or maybe only one. Our work permits didn't matter anymore. Nor did blue or green cards, our papers, our yellow stars, our submissive attitudes or our downcast eyes. This was the slaughter we had been hearing about for weeks, this was the massacre that we heard was coming. Only God could save us now. And we watched him closely: the god of the yellow gloves, the god of the bare flicking finger, the god who told you where to go – if you would live or die.

On each side of the square two lines of human misery faced each other with grim expressions and brutalized eyes. How do you face a row of condemned souls? How do you look them in the eye? How do you not resent them should they live? How do you not pity them should they die?

Behind us, in the background we could hear the familiar chugging of the German trucks as their engines shifted into idle, their exhaust pipes belching smoke in the chilly Polish morning, their drivers sitting impassively behind the wheel as if they were stopped at a traffic light.

No one knew what was going to happen to us. We waited and listened, watched and shivered and waited some more. And then, out of nowhere, the loudest Purim noisemaker of them all sounded the death knell for thousands of my fellow Jews.

At 8 a.m. exactly, a siren wailed from the German loudspeakers overhead and the slaughter began. With deadly efficiency the German soldiers and their eager accomplices started to load the military trucks with Jewish men, women and children who had been selected by the elegant-looking German civilians with their bare, pink, flicking fingers.

I was standing with my family in one such line, the next to be selected. As I advanced in the line, the debonair German civilian motioned for me to go to the left, which for the moment meant "life." Behind me, the man pointed to my father to go to the right. I was panicked, not believing what was happening. The horrors we had managed to escape, the terrors we had so far avoided, were crashing down upon the family Lato as the frozen sun slowly rose over the chaotic scene.

Then my father, as calmly and politely as possible, explained to the statuesque German that we were a family, that I was his son and that we should be together. I don't know if it was my father's gentle voice, his handsome face or the sincerity in his intelligent eyes, but the German allowed us to stay together. Once again our lives had been spared.

Others were not so lucky.

On the street, the people in lines stood peacefully, quietly awaiting their fate. Once ordered into the trucks, they still remained mute. I noticed the grim resignation as they stepped up into the trucks, shuffling toward the back, crowded shoulder to shoulder. Only when the gears shifted, only when the noisy German trucks lurched forward did their doomed human cargo begin to cry, to gag, to scream. Screams of fear, of anger, of hatred, of terror filled my head as they passed by, one after the other; the sounds of human wailing penetrating my soul.

Eventually I caught a quick flash of movement out of the corner of my eye. I strained in the early morning light hoping that what I was seeing was just a figment of my imagination, from the stress of trying to stay alive. But it was true. While I stood there with the rest of my family in the left line, I saw something truly unbelievable and shockingly inhumane.

A young, good-looking woman, perhaps in her mid-twenties, dressed in fine clothes and clearly pregnant by the size of her bulging belly, was killing little Jewish babies. As the doomed prepared to step into the military trucks on her side of the square, as they walked by shuffling toward their death, she would snatch a tiny infant from its mothers' arms and quickly smash its head against the side of the truck, killing it instantly in a blister of blood and gore as the parents watched in horror, held back by burly German soldiers and their deadly machine guns.

Again and again, her pale white fingers grabbed the chubby, pink feet of small infants – pulling them from their mothers' embrace – then slammed their little heads against the cold steel of the rear truck panels and tossed them into the pile of innocent human carnage slowly growing inside the truck. Toddlers and bigger children she shot with a pistol borrowed from a German soldier. When she ran out of bullets, a new soldier rushed over and handed her his gun so she would not lose her rhythm, not interrupt her killing spree for an instant. Again and again she emptied a casual bullet into a little girl's or a little boy's head as they were held up for her by the German soldiers.

While I stood there in the cold – it was perhaps ten degrees outside – I began to perspire from the fear and loathing. The selection process continued around us, never stopping, never ebbing. Jews were divided into left lines, then right lines, left, right, again and again. Families were separated, husbands and wives, brothers and sisters. It didn't matter. Into the trucks they went, driven off to meet their fate as they screamed out through the bars in the back of the doors.

The German soldiers, meanwhile, supervised the well-ordered chaos. Before my eyes the largest Jewish slaughter in the history of Baranowicze was carried out. As Jewish men prayed and Jewish women screamed, the pink fingers still pointed and flicked – left, right, right, left, live, die, die, live. For four long hours the Germans lined us up, divided us, then sent half away in rumbling military trucks to meet their deaths. Finally, precisely at noon, the overhead sirens sounded again and, just as quickly as it had started, the *first* slaughter of Baranowicze was over.

The Germans and their hateful allies left us standing bewildered and dazed, but alive, in the middle of the town square. On their way out, as an afterthought, they told us, "Go home."

That morning 3,600 Jewish people were killed. That

morning 3,600 men, women and children were exterminated; some before my very eyes. In four horrific hours on the joyous Jewish holiday of Purim, the Germans killed more than a third of the Jewish population in the Baranowicze ghetto.

It was over and, for the moment, my mother, my father and my brother were still alive. Our lives had been spared. There was hope. It was a fitting ninth birthday present for my brother. I had celebrated my seventeenth birthday a week earlier. As we walked slowly home from the bloodied town square, I couldn't help but think, Would it be my last?

# RESISTANCE

I had had enough. I started to seriously think about joining the ghetto resistance, the underground, which I had heard about.

There was no question that we would be next. In that *first* slaughter they wiped out 3,600 Jews from the ghetto. Before that they had randomly killed 1,500 Jews in roundups. Was there any question where they would go looking for victims for the next slaughter? I wasn't going to wait around. I decided to take action.

Without my parent's knowledge, I contacted several of my good friends to find out how to join this movement, this resistance. As soon as I did a whole world of information and secrecy opened to me. A secret language, too, and the minute I asked about it, I was suddenly given an interpreter to help me understand the reality of how life under military occupation worked.

My childhood was far behind me. It was time for fact, not fantasy. It was time for reality, not imagination. All around us, while my father and I had been shuffling off to work, while my brother and I had been snoring fitfully in our beds, another world had been operating. How had all this been going on right under my nose without my knowing? I was astounded.

Suddenly I discovered that many of my close friends were members of the resistance movement.

Suddenly I was in on the big secret. There was no looking back. For the first time in months – or years – I felt the faint stirrings of something unfamiliar fluttering around in my long, dead chest. That stirring was hope, reawakening from a long slumber.

I knew that without hope, one's soul is dead.

The process was slow and secretive. In order to avoid spies, to keep the Germans from knowing anything, the Jewish Resistance Movement turned out to be as smart and as secretive as the Nazis. First I contacted one of my friends. Next he introduced me to another member. And then another. From there I had to wait for the group to contact me. When they did, I was accepted. Suddenly I was a member of the Jewish Resistance Movement. A true freedom fighter. A soldier. A guerrilla.

In a rushed ceremony, I was sworn to complete secrecy. I could share nothing, say nothing, tell nothing to anyone. Not to my father, not to my mother, not to my brother, not to my extended family, not to my friends, not to my girlfriend, not to my neighbors. I could only share with other members, other *known* members of the resistance movement. Because of this, they had been able to keep the movement secret – and alive – for a long time.

I began attending secret meetings, surprised to see so many familiar faces huddled in the weak light of a flickering kerosene lamp in someone's barn, shed or even outhouse. I would never know how long they had been members, that was their secret.

Eventually we formed "cells," or groups of 10 people. Then meetings were only with our own cell, only for those 10 people. Most of the members of our cell were young people, and we met whenever we could spare a few minutes before curfew.

Our parents thought that we were just socializing, simply chatting and brought us water and stale bread for refreshments. We felt guilty keeping secrets from our parents, but to involve them might bring further harm – or disaster – to the very people we were trying to protect.

For safety reasons, the members of our cell didn't interact with members of other cells. Ever. That way, if one was caught, interrogated and forced to confess, only nine others would be implicated. The rest of the movement would go on. Everything was confidential, but I learned that about 20 cells were already operating in the ghetto. That meant there were 200 other Jews who were willing to fight the Germans.

As we anxiously awaited the inevitable *second* slaughter, our meetings grew more industrious, more useful and more urgent. We studied about resistance, underground work, and how to go on missions. The kerosene lamps burned and we stayed until the last minute before curfew to leave each other: excited, renewed and alive.

Before long I was ready for my first assignment. My first act of resistance, my first duty as a loyal, trusted and reliable Jewish Resistance Fighter: to smuggle four rifle bullets into the ghetto.

I was terrified. If caught smuggling bullets into the ghetto I would be shot on the spot. No questions asked: no interrogation, no trial, no jury. The stakes were terribly high, but I was convinced that I was going to die any day anyway. We all were.

Better to go down fighting, better to take some Nazis down with us than be slaughtered in our own homes, gunned down helplessly in our beds. That is what kept me alive, that is what made me brave enough to smuggle bullets passed five or six German guards when I would rather be playing ping-pong with my friends or holding hands with my girlfriend. That is what gave me the strength to go on.

When hope dies, when faith is murdered, only vengeance remains.

Over 5,100 Jews had already been senselessly massacred, brutally slaughtered. Not *one* German soldier had been killed, let alone wounded. What better way to start a resistance than with 4 bullets smuggled in by a pimply teenage kid?

I was still deathly afraid. I did not sleep the night before, nor eat the morning of the mission. I sweated beneath my clothes, my hands shook and my legs felt like jelly as I walked to work that day.

That afternoon I met with two girls in the laundry where my father worked; Jewish girls, forced to work, surviving with work permits, slaving away for the Germans.

But these two Jewish girls were different; special. These Jewish girls had boyfriends – special boyfriends – German soldiers who, because they saw these girls as human beings, as people, as individuals, decided to help. They disagreed with Hitler's superman philosophy and were disgusted by his violent and brutal acts against the Jews. It was from these sympathetic, young German soldiers that the bullets and, later on more supplies, would come. Of course no one in the laundry knew about it.

I picked up the bullets from the girls, frightened that my German foreman would find out, but even more frightened of what might happen if my father discovered my mission. He had no idea I was a member of the resistance. No idea I was going to risk my life smuggling four bullets into the ghetto. If he had, he would have fainted from fear, but only after exploding with anger. My father never would have allowed me risk my life in such a way, even for such a noble cause as the Jewish resistance. Rather, he would have tied me to the bunk bed at home and never let me out of the house.

The two girls in the laundry were smart. They had made special sashes to tie around my ankles. One bullet went on one side of my ankle, another bullet on the other side. They secured them with bandages, then wound the sashes tightly around the four bullets and covered them with my thick woolen socks which were folded over the top of my boots.

Spot checks were more frequent these days, but most of the time the Germans ignored the lower part of your legs. Too many Jews to pat down, too far to bend over to feel their socks, to touch their "dirty Jew shoes." Besides, what Jew would be brave enough or dumb enough to risk his or her life smuggling something inside the ghetto? With so many guards watching? Under the threat of instant death?

Though I knew my socks looked no different on this particular day than any other, I felt as if the whole town was staring at my ankles. I walked a death march back to the ghetto that evening after work, my father, I'm sure, wondering why I was so quiet, so preoccupied. Then, with my breath held and my heart beating double time, I made it through the guards at the gate without incident.

I don't know how I did it. Later that night I handed the bullets to a member of my cell and that was the last I saw of them. I felt very proud of what I had accomplished. I had helped the resistance. No matter how small an effort it was, I had helped to fight back.

Once the initial fear and nervousness wore off, missions such as these became almost routine. In the coming weeks, I smuggled in more bullets. Always 4 at a time, always with the bandages, then the sashes, then the socks. On another occasion, I smuggled in badly needed medicine. For this, the two girls in the laundry made a special sash to go around my waist. It looked like a cummerbund from a tuxedo. On one side was cotton padding, so if the soldiers at the gate patted my belly they wouldn't feel its contents. On the other side were small pockets that had been sewn in it, one next to the other, for the purpose of smuggling in vials of morphine or tablets of aspirin.

I swelled with pride each time I passed by the unsuspecting guards and through the gate. I looked around at the other workers as they said goodnight and split off to return to their various homes. Which were cell members? I wondered, Was it that one with the funny hat? Or that one with the beard? What had they just smuggled in? Were their hearts still pounding like mine? How long had it been going on? How many nights had I walked in carrying nothing? How many bullets could I have smuggled? Or morphine? How much time had I wasted before finding the courage to join the cause? How many lives could I have saved? These thoughts flooded my head.

Some missions were more dangerous than others.

One time I had to walk on the sidewalks of Baranowicze posing as a gentile, without my stars or any identification papers on my person. I met a man, a contact in the city, who gave me a gun, which I then smuggled into the laundry where my father worked. Luckily it was up to someone else to actually smuggle the gun into the ghetto.

Other times I only smuggled my cigarette lighters or printed material bearing information from our gentile contacts in town. A map here. Instructions there. A date, a warning, a news bulletin.

There was a network of Jewish sympathizers working from within – and without – the Jewish Resistance Movement. Some were Jewish, some were gentile and some were German soldiers, like our friends at the laundry. Unless they were from your cell, unless you sat across from them in cramped and hurried, nightly meetings, you didn't know who was on your side or who was against you. It was both frustrating and exhilarating. But I had a life. A reason to go on.

We faced life and death every single day. Smuggling,

plotting, planning, hiding, sneaking and stealing. Frightening, but exciting. It was risking death to live life. Whenever we left someone's house in those days, instead of "Goodnight," "Until we meet again" or "Shalom," we would always say half-jokingly, "If I live, I'll see you tomorrow. If not, I'll see you the day after."

At our nightly meetings before curfew came, the members of our cell and I scrutinized every scrap of news, true or made-up, about the German *"aktions"* on the Eastern front. We had no radios. All we had was German newspapers, which we had also smuggled in from the laundry and which were naturally slanted in favor of Hitler and the German army:

"GERMANY WINS AGAIN!"
"HITLER TRIUMPHANT!"

We learned to interpret the newspapers by reading between the lines. We compared the differences between the news from the previous week with the news of the present week. We analyzed tiny details, inconsistencies, hidden phrases and came to our own conclusions. The Germans did not always win; the Germans were not always triumphant. In fact by this time it appeared that the German offensive had slowed down to almost a standstill on the Eastern front. There was some hope after all, but my friends and I knew that we could no longer wait for the allies to storm in to save us. We had learned that if we were to be saved, we would have to save ourselves.

After the Purim slaughter, the summer of 1942 was a grim, bleak period of suspense and tortuous tedium. Life went on. We worked. We ate. We slept. I smuggled. There were "minor" killings, if you could call them that. But not too many more roundups, or Jews being pulled off the streets and forced into slave labor. But as summer faded into fall and the trees shed their lush, green foliage, more rumors began to fly.

Disturbing rumors, not just about a coming slaughter, another massacre, but about Jews being beaten or killed at work.

Now my father and I faced each day with a new sense of dread: not sure we would be safe at work. In the morning none of us knew whether we would ever see each other again. My mother and my little brother Jackob stayed close to the house, just in case an *aktion* or attack should begin while we were at work.

We never really knew. It was very frustrating, very depressing. My smuggling operations, our nightly cell meetings, were the only events in my life that I looked forward to.

One day I walked home from work in a column with the H.K.P. workers. It so happened that I was walking next to a girl who worked in the laundry. She was about my age and fairly new. I really did not know if this was just a coincidence, or whether she arranged it to meet me. I didn't care. We started talking to each other and before we realized it we had reached the ghetto. We promised to keep company, walking to and from work together. She was attractive and pleasant to talk to. Her name was Sima, and we became friends.

After awhile, we began to see each other more often. We became boyfriend and girlfriend. I was seventeen and she was eighteen.

Being a member of the ghetto's resistance and having a girlfriend meant that my life became more bearable and it was easier to cope with everyday uncertainties.

Our relationship quickly blossomed. However, because of the unbelievable circumstances facing us under the German occupation, we realized, understood and agreed that we had to be very careful. It was not right for us to be too intimate, except for holding hands, an occasional hug or a kiss. We were young and eager but each day presented an uncertain future.

She did not know I belonged to the ghetto resistance movement. She did not know that I had rifle bullets attached to my legs while walking home.

# THE SECOND SLAUGHTER

*Rosh Hashanah 1942*

After the first slaughter, my father, my uncle and a few of the other men from our cramped ghetto apartment decided to build a secret bunker in the basement under our house. We were not the only ones. Bunkers sprang up all over the ghetto, anywhere they could. We had to do something, anything, to improve our odds of survival in preparation for the next assault.

With the Germans, there was always more death and destruction looming. Our hope was that we could finish the bunker before the next *aktion*, the next massacre.

The bunker was designed to hold 4 families, 16 people. And that was stretching it to the limits of human endurance. The space would be small, the air would be rank, the walls would drip with humidity and sweat, but survival was all that mattered. The adult men started to dig immediately after the Purim slaughter.

As spring blossomed a problem arose: What to do with the dug-up sand?

The problem was solved by making the floor in the basement a little bit higher. In the space between the basement floor and the bunker roof, they stowed away the sand. Not only would this make the basement floor itself less hollow, which would keep the Germans from getting suspicious as they trampled across it in their shiny boots, but it would also make more room in the bunker.

The work was hard, long and exhausting. The men would start digging as soon as they got home at night and work until they passed out from fatigue. If they stayed home sick, they dug between racking coughs. Over the weekend they dug between

Temple and their afternoon nap. It took all of April, May, June, July and even part of August to finish the grueling job. When the bunker was ready, when it had grown as large as it possibly could, we scrounged a week's worth of food in case we had to hide in the earthen shelter. At that moment, because we had a place to hide, we felt just a little bit safer.

The six months between Purim and Rosh Hashanah had barely passed when, on September 22, the *second* slaughter of Baranowicze began.

The day began as usual, with my mother and brother waving to us as my father and me trudged our way to the front gate for work. But by 7 a.m. they had sealed the ghetto once again.

Even before we got there, we could tell that something was wrong. There were women who were screaming and men who were praying. Through the gleaming barbed wire fence we saw the guards who escorted us to work still standing outside the ghetto gate, grim-faced and unyielding.

The air was electric, full of fear and suspicion, already hinting at impending doom. The wailing, the crying, the screaming, sent us into a panic and we knew that another slaughter was about to occur. My father and I dashed back to the house, grabbed my mother and brother, whatever extra food we had and raced to hide in the bunker.

By 8 a.m. 21 of us had crammed ourselves into the L-shaped bunker, our bodies rested against each other, elbow to kneecap, our feet digging into the hard-packed, earthen floor, sweat beading on our brows, under our arms, on our chests, as the body heat from almost two dozen people quickly sucked the air out of the tiny space. There was barely enough room in the bunker for so many people, but who could we kick out? Who could we force to leave? How could we live with ourselves if we asked someone to leave so we could be a bit more comfortable?

A well in the backyard abutted one corner of the bunker. The men thought that by drilling a hole in it they could accomplish two goals: bring in some much-needed fresh air and perhaps devise a way to siphon out some fresh water. But the hole was too small to provide more air.

We suffered in that bunker, but not nearly as much as they suffered above ground. Through all that dirt between our heads and the basement floor, and through the walls of the house above us, we could hear the gunfire, hear the sirens, hear the screaming, hear the cries for help as Jews were being massacred by the Germans.

The first day stretched on and on. When the shooting, the screaming and the fighting stopped, the ghetto became eerily quiet. Then, just as suddenly, it would start back up: twice as viciously, twice as ferociously. Underground, 21 of us sat elbow to elbow, thigh to thigh, taking shallow breaths, trying to conserve air as neighbors, friends and family were killed above us.

With so many people packed inside, the bunker was quickly transformed into a sweltering oven and we were forced to undress to survive. We sat naked, whole families, men and women next to each other, across from one another, our bare flesh pushed up against each other as the sweat continued to pour down faces, chests, backs and thighs. The pail we shared overflowed.

Finally after four torturous and endless days, a small group of us were unable to take it any longer. That's when 5 of us, a young couple in their twenties, two of my teenage friends and me, decided to risk leaving the bunker to breathe fresh air and, perhaps, find help from the gentiles of Baranowicze.

At two in the morning we crept back into our sweaty, sodden clothes and slowly, fearfully, crawled from the sweaty dank bowels of the humid bunker. We glanced at the destruction, the broken dishes, hanging cupboards and shattered glass in our house, then stole into the darkened, quiet streets, gulping down fresh air, the breeze drying our sweaty bodies as we ran.

The ghetto was destroyed and deserted; the gates reopened, perhaps as a ruse, perhaps by neglect. We thought it might be a trick. We thought the Germans might simply be drawing us out into the open. But we fled through the gates anyway, hiding outside the ghetto in a burned-out house until daylight. Then we went to our gentile friends, knocking on their doors, hoping to find relief, rescue and comfort from our old friends and neighbors.

But they slammed their doors in our faces. We were spat on, berated, harassed, humiliated and rejected. Once we thought of these people as friends; now we worried they might turn us in. My friends and I decided to return to the ghetto and face death together with our families.

As we treaded our way back, it was decided that one of us would walk on the sidewalk to scout for Germans while the rest of us would sneak into the ghetto through various backyards. When all was clear, the last brave volunteer would smuggle himself back in; that is, if he were still alive.

I looked like a gentile, so I was chosen to be the lookout. With my youthful height, ruddy looks and stocky build, I looked the least like a starving, ghetto-living Jew. And so, off came my stars, out went my papers and onto the sidewalk I turned while my friends scurried through the brush to make it back to safety.

It was not long before I was approached by a German policeman.

The policemen were different than the soldiers but just as menacing. The powers of the police were less official, though no less deadly, and my fear was no less diminished by the slight distinction.

"Papers?" he asked suspiciously in German.

"Where is your star?" he demanded when it became obvious that I was a Jew.

I had no answers for this angry man blocking my path.

Enraged, he took his rifle and poked me in the chest with its cold, steel barrel. Backing me up with the rifle, he stopped when I was dead up against a light pole, the rifle's muzzle pressing into my chest.

But the policeman could not leave his post. He said that when his replacement came, which was in a few moments, he would take me to the local police precinct and execute me personally.

I knew he meant it. The Gestapo, the central police headquarters, was in what had been my Aunt Rosa's home before the war. A beautiful home, full of elegant rooms divided into apartments for family members or privileged tenants. Picturesque and centrally located, on the main street of Baranowicze's once-lovely town square, the Germans had quickly requisitioned it upon the invasion.

Out back, where once was a beautiful orchard where my brother and I picked fresh apples, now stood a bleak and blood-stained brick wall where the German police lined up and gunned down Jews whose only sin was being caught on the street without a yellow star or hiding a crust of bread in their pocket. Now this was to be my fate as well. How my aunt would wail to learn I was executed in her own orchard!

Time slowed as the rifle muzzle bore into my chest. I remember the look on the policeman's vengeful face, the smell of nicotine on his breath, the light of the street lamp in the early evening making him look cartoonish, somehow out of focus, as I waited to die. Time ticked by, I don't know how long, maybe seconds, maybe minutes, maybe hours, before a German soldier approached.

This is it, I thought. His replacement is here. Now I am going to my aunt's house, now I am signing my name in the book of death.

I only hoped that I could be brave for my family, that I could take it like a man and not cry or piss in my pants.

Instead the German soldier pushed the rifle barrel away from my chest and railed at the policeman, who was his subordinate. On the streets of Baranowicze, no one had power like the German soldiers.

The soldier pointed at me, called me "Mein Jude" (my Jew), and asked why this policeman thought he had the right to keep me when all along he had been waiting for me to come to the professional shop.

The German soldier punched me lightly on the shoulder and scolded me good-naturedly for forgetting my star and walking on the sidewalk. He dismissed the policeman, then sent me home. Back into the ghetto. Alive.

Later on I learned that a group of Jewish professionals – tailors, shoemakers and jewelers – had been working late into the evening just across from the ghetto gate in the trades building, trying to fill a special order. Inside the shop a tailor was rushing to finish a suit for a German soldier who was waiting. From the window the tailor saw me being accosted by the policeman. Thinking quickly, he told the German soldier he would give him the suit as a gift if he would go across the street and rescue me from the policeman.

The German soldier did just that. I never knew his name or even the name of the tailor. I don't know what special occasion the suit was for. I had been marked for death, but I was still alive and trudging back to the ghetto to my family.

I found my family in a nearby apartment. When the killing was finally over, they had left the bunker and found solace with several friends. They had some straw on the floor with a black cover on it and were saying prayers for the dead, the *Kaddish*. There were two candles lit on each side. They were sitting *shiva* for someone. But for whom? I frowned, thinking one of my friends had not made it back alive, or perhaps the bunker had been discovered and someone had been shot in cold blood. I spoke, asking who had died and watched my family turn around shocked but relieved to see me standing in the doorway. The funeral I was interrupting was my own! When I heard that, I just burst out crying. Oh, how I cried.

My friends returning to the ghetto had seen me accosted by the German policeman, thought for sure that I had been killed and told my family the sad news.

Imagine crying at your own funeral.

That night we slept fitfully. Was the slaughter over? Had it even begun? In the morning, the Nazis used the loudspeakers to tell us that the *aktion* was over, that we could come out of the bunkers and go to work.

My father and I did not believe them and dreaded leaving my mother and my little brother behind, but what could we do? The Germans expected us to work. It was the only way to stay alive.

At the gate, however, one of the German soldiers who escorted us to the factory every day, whispered to my father that the *aktion* was *not* over, that the *real* slaughter had only just begun. He told my father that the commandant had ordered him to get my family and a few others and together they would bring us into the factory until the slaughter was over. They were protecting us because we were "Their Jews!"

Quickly we grabbed my mother and my little brother and the others and took them with us. Silently we dashed through the ghetto, out the gate, escorted by this befriending soldier who turned us over to our German foreman. That German fed us and hid us from the Nazis, saving us as the *second* slaughter raged on inside the ghetto.

It took the Germans seven days to kill almost all the Jews left in the Baranowicze ghetto. Meanwhile we worked, hid, ate and slept in the relative safety of the factory. Later we heard how cruelly the Germans had executed those unfortunate Jews.

First they had routed the Jews from their homes. Kicking down doors, breaking windows, spraying walls with gunfire. Closets were kicked in, attics pulled down and many hiding Jews discovered.

They found them in crawl spaces and under beds. They found children in dresser drawers. Wherever a body could fit – young, old, short, tall, thin, fat – they hid. But the Germans found them anyway.

When the killing stopped and houses grew quiet, the Germans listened for the sounds of Jews running to safety, whispering to each other across a shattered room, or creaking ever so quietly as they shifted their hindquarters or stretched their cramped legs. Then a lethal spray of machine-gun fire would erupt and the deadly game of hide and seek was over.

The houses were easy prey compared to the bunkers. The family Lato had not been alone in their industriousness. Many Jewish families inside the ghetto had dug bunkers both big and small. Some were easier to find than others, some more difficult. When the Germans tired of going under basements, getting dirt under their nails, dust in their hair or sod on their precious uniforms, they bribed the gentiles of Baranowicze into helping. Civilian men, women and children officially deputized by the German soldiers to root out human life, wound through the ghetto eagerly to hunt us down. With zeal they found the Jews, sniffing out bunkers with deadly accuracy. They reported Jews with glee, pointing to families uncovered, ignoring their cowering protestations, increasing their tallies as the days mounted. For every Jew the gentiles found, they received a packet of tobacco. For every two Jews, a bonus – a bottle of vodka! Such was the price of a life.

Eventually the Germans had enough of the killing, enough of the massacre. The *second* slaughter was over. The German commandant at the factory told us it was okay to go home. What do you say to someone who has saved your life? What do you say when you are alive knowing so many others are dead? In the end, we just left. There were no words.

In the ghetto our temporary home had been completely destroyed. We were left with the clothes on our back, the clothes we had slept in the first night of the *second* slaughter, the clothes my mother and brother had worn to wave us off to work that morning. There had been no time to hide silver in our socks or family photos in our underwear. We had lost everything, but we were *still* alive.

Of the 13,000 Jews who had been crammed into the Baranowicze ghetto, only 600 remained. We joined them in our shrunken ghetto, in our dwindling Jewish section as the grisly figures slowly came in: In 7 days, between September 22 and the 29th, in an orgy of mayhem, terror and death, the Germans had decimated 6,200 Jews – men, women and children.

# ESCAPE

After the *second* slaughter, the Germans began closing off the old ghetto and making a new, smaller ghetto. We were told that we could find houses for ourselves. After all, what did it matter to the Germans where we lived? They were going to kill us eventually.

Now a full member of the Jewish Resistance Movement, I found an apartment next to my family where I could be close, but also live with my new friends in the cell. This was quite a shock to my parents, but things were different now, for all of us. They could keep an eye on me, watch over me, kiss me goodnight, yet let me have my independence. I was still their son, but no longer their little boy. My father had realized this the day that he had caught me smoking.

Living with friends from my cell allowed us to plan more efficiently, more progressively. As the summer ended and fall began, as the peace and quiet of life in the "new" ghetto was fractured with new rumors, we began planning our escape in earnest. Our smuggling increased. We pressed our contacts for an extra rifle, gun or a couple of grenades, but were not successful in our attempts to arm ourselves. We continued to go to work every day, looking like everybody else in the grim and gritty ghetto. The last thing we wanted to do when our goal was so close was to arouse suspicion.

We heard that members of other cells had already left the ghetto, escaped to the forests outside Baranowicze and joined Russian partisans rumored to be scattered there, fighting the Germans however they could. We grew excited at this news, the thought of teaming up with other resistance fighters – with Russian partisans no less – to hurt the Germans, damage their airfields, sabotage their railways, maybe even kill a few while we were at it.

We decided to run before it was too late. Before we were dead like all the others. Before they had a chance to slaughter us. We consulted our calendars, read the German papers more intently, listened for signals and finally decided upon the day to leave – it would be October 9, 1942. We would run to the forests, join other cells, link up with the Russian partisans and learn guerrilla warfare in the woods that we had played in as little children.

One of the guys in our cell had established a rapport with one of the guards at the ghetto fence. Somehow we had managed to come up with one gold ten-ruble piece with which to bribe him. After intense negotiations over several days, the guard finally agreed. The decision came so fast that there was no time to alert our families, no time to say goodbye.

Without my father's permission, I grabbed his winter coat, a few other supplies and just left.

We assembled our cell, gathered up our things. We had instructions where to meet our contacts outside the gate. Blinking away the tears in our eyes, we walked through the ghetto knowing that we might never see our families again.

I thought of my father, so proud of me all his life. What would he think when he came to get me for work the next morning? Would he be disappointed? Or proud? And my mother? I knew she would cry, perhaps for days on end. My little brother, too. He would think I had deserted him. So young, so innocent, he would probably hate me forever. I would miss them all terribly. My stomach was knotted with fear and regret.

Ten o'clock came. We gave the guard the ten rubles and he spread the barbed wire fence just wide enough for us to get through. And we left the Baranowicze ghetto.

One minute we were inside, the next minute we were outside. It was as simple and final as that.

There were 16 of us standing outside the ghetto fence that night, my whole cell and a few friends. We ran into the darkness as fast as we could. After a while we stopped, got our bearings and started to walk toward our rendezvous.

We were so excited, so free, that we never turned our heads to look back.

# Part 4
# The Partisans

"TO STAY ALIVE, OUR RESOLUTION.
THAT WE WERE ALIVE,
OUR CELEBRATION."

– Partisan Motto

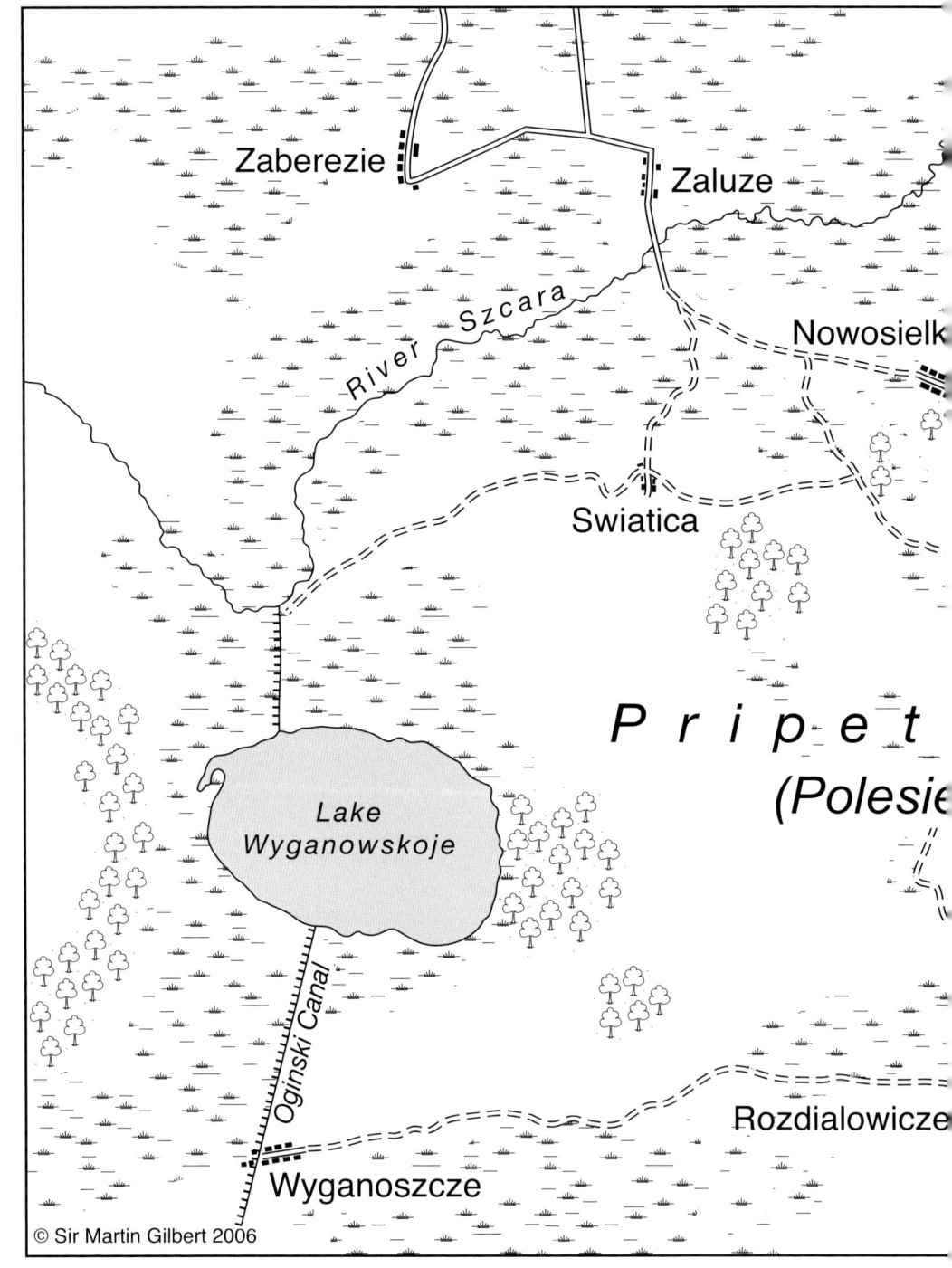

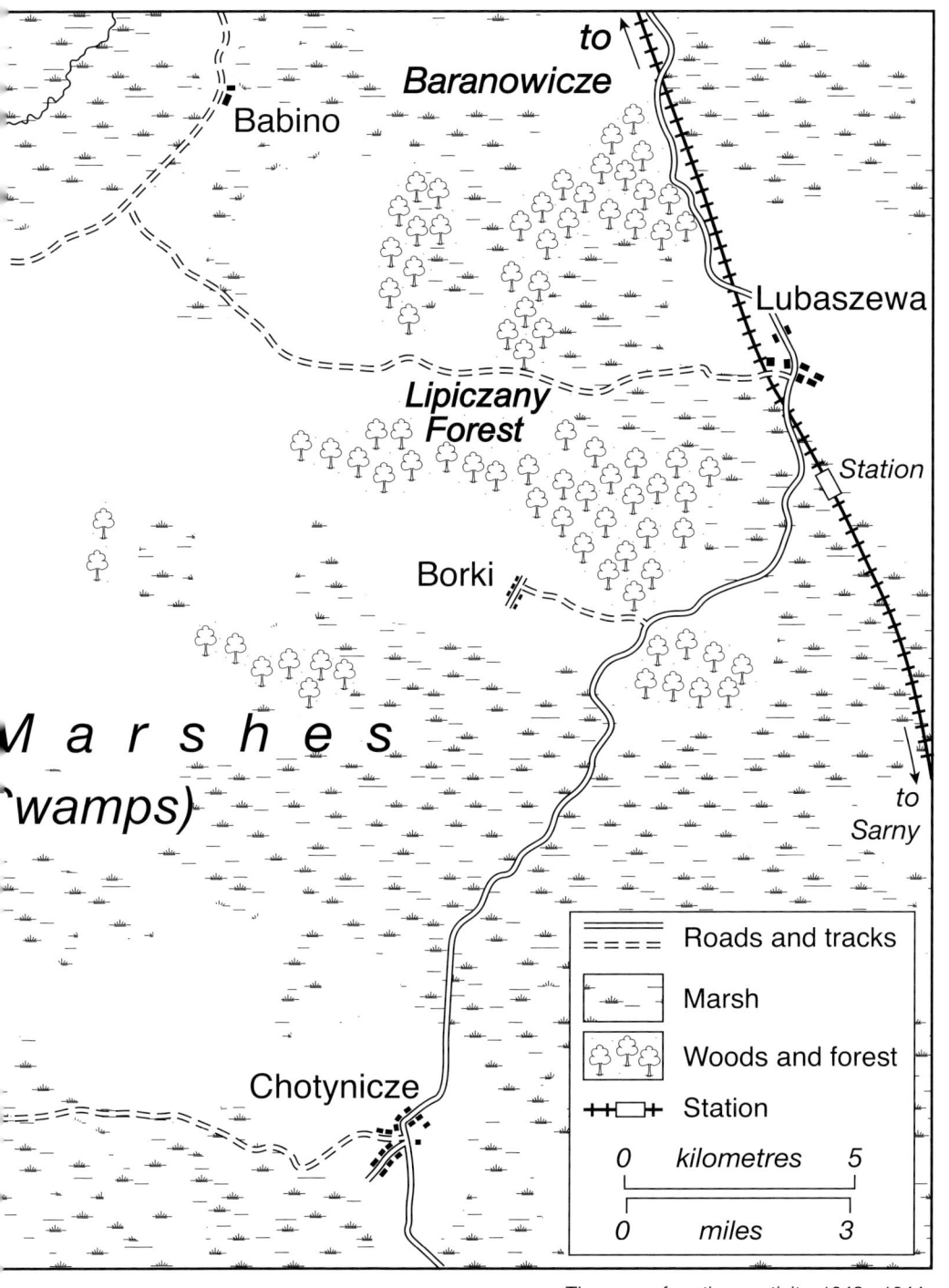

The area of partisan activity, 1942 - 1944.

# THE 10TH LOCK

The initial rush of freedom was exhilarating. The fresh forest air and the sound of crickets chirping during our escape was thrilling. To see the moon and stars above towering pines and birches, instead of over that 7-foot barbed wire fence that surrounded the ghetto for 18 months, was truly liberating.

The night was cold and damp, and the October chill cut through our thin ghetto clothes even as the harsh ground tore into the heel of our bumbling work shoes. We stumbled, fell and got back up again as we wandered through the night searching for our contact, the guide who would indoctrinate us into the secret world of forest living and guerrilla warfare in the Lipiczany Forest, also known as the Polesie swamps.

We had instructions to go southwest from the ghetto in the direction of the 10th lock (canal) into the swampy, unfamiliar jungle that made up the Lipiczany Forest, supposedly under partisan control. Somehow, somewhere, by mentioning the words "10th lock," a certain farmer was supposed to know where to contact the partisans on our behalf.

We stumbled on gamely in the vague direction of south by southwest, although it was difficult to get our bearings in the dark Polish night. After being cooped up and confined in the Baranowicze ghetto for so long, to be finally off and running was hard to get used to. My legs cramped, hindering me.

We were headed toward the territory full of well-hidden swamps near the Polish villages of Swiatica and Zaluze: To the Lipiczany Forest, where we were to be lodged and trained and where we would eventually accomplish most of our missions. The Forest was located between the Polish cities of Vilna, Bialystok and Pinsk.

We kept going, breathing in the cold night air and getting

scratched by wayward branches. Our cell leader was a young man with former military experience called "Kubus." He was about twenty-five years old. He seemed much wiser than his years and on that particular evening and in the many days and nights that would follow, he was nothing short of our savior.

I learned that Kubus had obtained the ten gold rubles for bribing the ghetto guard from leaders of the resistance movement. Now he was leading 16 smooth-faced greenhorns through the dark forest night to safety, secrecy and a different kind of danger.

It was no easy task.

Kubus led us in the general direction of a nearby airfield, where he would be able to get his bearings.

It took us a long time to get used to the darkness. In the inky night that enveloped us I had to watch my feet to make sure I didn't step in a ditch or a hole and twist my ankle, sabotaging the entire operation.

From the airfield we followed the road out of town. Though Kubus had directions and was following them as well as he could, we still got lost. In the bowels of darkness it was impossible to follow the road, see the landmarks, count off paces or follow any kind of map whatsoever.

We walked all night long and missed our contact, whom we were supposed to meet at 1 a.m. A cottage near the airstrip was where we had been headed, but it was impossible to find. Thus began our two-week journey.

Tired, nervous, fearful, hungry and lost, we wound up at a secluded spot by the edge of the forest. To our disappointment, the forest foliage was merely shrubs, not the dense trees we had expected and would have preferred. Worse yet, the spot was not far from a German post. Dawn was quickly approaching and we didn't need Kubus to tell us that walking around in the daytime would be suicide.

The sun soon rose and revealed new details. Not only were we near a post crawling with German soldiers, we were practically on top of it!

Now it was too late to move, for fear of discovery and certain death.

And it was only our first day!

By eight in the morning we could hear German soldiers talking – that was how close we were to them – and their vicious attack dogs sniffing, growling and barking. At first we thought they had spotted us. All we could do was wait, camouflaged by a cover of thin shrubs, shivering in the cold and weak from hunger on our first night's journey outside of the ghetto.

We waited and waited, but nothing happened. Then the dogs started barking again, moving in our direction. We could hear their low, guttural growls. They inched closer and closer, their big furry paws trampling twigs as they moved steadily toward our hiding spot. Behind them, German soldiers.

We were convinced that we would be captured and strung up for the residents of the Baranowicze ghetto to see.

An example of what happens to Jews who try to escape.

A German mockery of pitiful Jewish bravery.

A warning to those who might be thinking of running.

As the women cried into their hands and the men prayed silently, I began to regret leaving the ghetto. Not only would I die a horrible, miserable death surrounded by strangers instead of my family, but I hadn't yet done a single thing to advance the cause of the resistance. I had only escaped certain death in the ghetto for a *more* certain death in the forest.

Seconds became minutes then, literally, hours. We sat perfectly still and quiet, our shoulders and necks stiff from covering, our haunches numb from the cold damp earth.

Suddenly the dogs barked then sped off in the opposite direction, their German masters trailing behind. It was nothing short of a miracle.

We were alone again.

Silent, cold, petrified, but alone.

They never returned during that long, miserable day. Although we still heard sounds of harsh German voices, we assumed that they were soldiers working on the nearby railroad. They were so close to us that we had to lay there in the shrubs all day. No food, no water, no coughing, no sneezing, no moving and certainly no talking.

We played dead, hiding behind that straggly line of winter-bare shrubs. October is harsh and the sunlight did little to thaw the hard, cold ground beneath our frost-bitten backs. Frigid steam filled the air as we took shallow breaths.

When it got dark the Germans left. After an hour of silence, we started to move. Slowly at first, our muscles and joints swollen and stiff from the long first night of our escape. We got our bearings and headed back into the frosty night.

Our first day of freedom was an initiation into the dangerous world of forest living.

As the second day began we trudged on blindly, muffling the sounds of our growling bellies with our hands.

Not long into our journey we noticed a single cottage in the distance. Kubus and one other brave man in our party volunteered to go see if the farmer who lived there might possibly help us with directions. It sounded simple, but it was no less dangerous than escaping from the ghetto or evading German guard dogs in the frozen, naked brush.

Every step we took was a mission; every mile was a battle, every breath another triumph. We were in uncertain territory, never knowing who was with us or who was against us.

To approach a strange family was to court disaster. The occupants could be helpful partisan sympathizers or deadly German spies. We had no way of knowing if the peasants would point us in the direction of partisan camps or straight into the path of the Germans.

Fortunately this farmer and his family were sympathetic to us. They gave us two loaves of bread, a little smoked bacon and a few boiled potatoes – our first meal in over twenty-four hours. We divided it evenly, then devoured it ravenously.

Our stomachs yearned for more.

If we thought the daily rations inside the Baranowicze ghetto were bad, finding food on our own each day was even worse. This helpful peasant family also gave us information that would help us find the 10th lock.

After our meal and a brief rest, we began walking again. Still, we couldn't find signs of any local partisan activity. Despite our map, Kubus' military experience and the new directions, at the end of our second long night of freedom we wound up just around the corner from the very place we had started from. We realized that if we didn't know our way in the forest, we would walk in circles. So far we had walked almost ten miles, most of them in circles.

We slept on the cold, hard ground huddled together for warmth, taking turns at the watch.

Each day we repeated our trek, making little headway, even losing ground. For our protection and safety, we tried to keep a tight line should anything happen and we had to stop suddenly, crouch down and take cover.

At some point during the fourth night, we lost a couple from our group, a husband and wife in their mid-twenties. One minute they were among us; in the next they had vanished into thin air. By the time we noticed they were gone, no one could remember last seeing them. They could have been anywhere, gone anywhere.

We were helpless to do anything about it. So we ground on, our cell smaller by two and lacking a grenade they had with them. Between the 14 of us, we had one rifle, one pistol and three grenades.

By the fifth night the harvest moon was full, making it easier to find our way; less bruises from tree trunks, fewer scratches on our face from errant branches. We trudged on stubbornly, making careful headway, though teetering from starvation, exhaustion and fear. We came across a well-tended field, where farmers had started to harvest rows and rows of leafy cabbage.

Ravenously we clawed at the cold, hard earth with our bare hands. At first I didn't understand why we were digging. I thought to myself, Why not just grab the head of cabbage and run? But the older people in the group explained that to survive you didn't just take food for one night, you stocked up on as much food as you could for the nights to come.

The rounded, bulky cabbage heads would take up too much space, they explained. Better to dig deeper and find the long, slender roots just beneath the bulky heads. These were long and thin, but full of concentrated food. They could be easily slipped into pockets, pant legs and knapsacks and took up a quarter of the room that cabbage heads did.

To satisfy our gnawing, aching hunger, we carefully cleaned the soil off several roots apiece and ate them, hunkered down at the edge of the freshly harvested field. With the bitter taste of the roots in our mouths, the grit of the sand still stuck between our teeth, we trudged on with more resolve, our hunger temporarily satisfied, our determination renewed. We walked all night, eager to find the partisans, eager to stop running and begin fighting.

---

Night after night we walked, stumbling and hoping. Day after day we slept, crouching and fearful. The pride and success we had felt at the beginning of our journey had faded away into grim routine.

It was hard to feel proud, wise or strong while lost with 14 other ghetto refugees, clinging to our threadbare clothes, shabby shoes and gritty, bitter cabbage roots.

It was easy to slip back into the more familiar feelings of fear, doom and dread.

I wondered if my father had been punished when I hadn't shown up with him for work the next morning. Had my mother and brother succumbed to a roundup? Had there been another *aktion*, another massacre?

We had had no news of our loved ones since the night we left the ghetto. Anything could have happened. It was hard not to feel guilty, even though it our goal had been to escape the ghetto to join the resistance, gather allegiances, form a regiment and return to save our families, not abandon them.

All thoughts of glory were left behind during those frigid, hungry nights. Now we just struggled onward stubbornly, resigned to survive in the forest as long as we could. Marching alongside, hunger was our constant companion. The October air was growing colder every night and the freezing hours just before dawn were bitterly and bitingly cold. So far we had managed to survive on the bread and bacon those first friendly farmers had given us, and a few pockets full of sandy, raw cabbage roots.

The Germans were everywhere, all around us, night and day. We saw them and, when they weren't in sight, we heard them. Their dogs barked and their curses flew as we stole past in the forest, inches from discovery.

We passed farmhouses and cottages, but could not risk approaching them.

All that time, all those risky nights, all those sleepless days, we never lost our burning will to survive. We walked together every night, slept together every day, watching each other's backs, dragging each other along. The longer we survived, the more determined we became.

There was always a tomorrow. Each night we were closer to our goal.

On the tenth night, we reached our first roadblock, our first impasse.

So far we had mainly traveled along overgrown paths deep in the forest. Now we faced a river, a moving body of water to cross if we were to reach our destination.

There was no way to cross this river. It was rather wide and looked formidable in the freezing October moonlight. Somebody spotted a small boat on the opposite riverbank. In our group, only Kubus knew how to swim.

Fearless and without regard for his own safety, Kubus swam across the river and brought the tiny dinghy back to shore. He nearly froze that night, braving the treacherous waters that were almost zero in temperature, fighting the current with his young, muscular arms, across then back.

The dinghy only had room for four people, so we crossed the river in shifts, four over, one back, until all of us had reached the other side safely and where Kubus sat, wet and shivering.

We were exhilarated as we left the dinghy and the riverbank behind, proud of our ingenuity and teamwork. Now we were in strange, new terrain, but closer to our destination. Crossing that river had given us inner strength.

Daylight came and we hunkered down in yet another encampment. Exhausted from our travels, but refreshed by our latest triumph, we slept deeply.

There was electricity in the air as we headed out that evening, our eleventh night, no longer 14 strangers, but a squad, a unit, a team.

By now we had shed most of our initial fear. We decided that this was a fairly safe area, no village in sight and not too far from the forest should we encounter unfriendly inhabitants.

We approached a large cottage and stopped.

The farmer and his family welcomed us inside and fed us cabbage soup with kielbasa, boiled potatoes and bread. We gorged ourselves, warmed by the food, the fire and the first hospitality in over a week.

For dessert they gave us something better than cake – directions to help us find the elusive Russian partisans. We left that friendly cottage happier than we had been in weeks. We decided to settle down for the rest of the night and the next day to rest our full bellies and make sense of the new directions.

After the day's rest, we felt prepared to face a new night – our twelfth on the long and arduous journey. Again, electricity charged the chill air as we awoke, stretched ourselves and limbered up for the long night's walk. It helped that we were rested and that we had been fed.

We started walking following our new directions, eager to face the dark of night. We walked for a long time before we stopped to rest.

Suddenly we heard noises. Everyone fell to the ground, listened and watched. Twigs crackled, leaves rustled and, suddenly, a big surprise! We couldn't believe our eyes – the couple we had lost ten nights earlier! We ran to them, surrounded them and welcomed them back.

They appeared dizzy, weak from exhaustion and hunger. We gave them some leftover bread and cabbage roots and decided to stop for the night to give them a chance to rest. We rejoiced for the two lost sheep returned to the fold.

The thirteenth night and day passed. On the fourteenth night, we began walking, still following the directions the generous peasants had given us.

That evening we stopped at another cottage.

We mentioned the 10th lock and the peasant told us where it was. They fed us and then sent us on our way with the warmest of wishes.

It was heartening to find such genuine goodness in people after experiencing heartache, anger, hatred and death for so very long.

As dawn broke on our fourteenth day, exactly two weeks, the first sight that met our eyes was 16 dead German soldiers littering the ground. Eyes still open, blood frozen on the ground, limbs askew. German soldiers were not invincible after all. They *could* be killed. Indeed, had been killed.

Suddenly there was rustling and movement among the trunks and branches. Several rough and haggard men appeared, then approached us cautiously, warily. They questioned us thoroughly and when they learned that we had escaped from the Baranowicze ghetto, they said that a lot of Jews from our town had fled and joined them.

They were Jewish partisans.

They shook our hands, embraced us warmly and told us to follow them.

We learned that the 10th lock was a secret code name for farmers and peasant sympathizers to determine who was legitimate and who was a spy.

At the first sound of 10th lock, the first farmers had informed the partisans that we were in the area. Immediately they set out to find us. Along the way they encountered the 16 German soldiers and killed them.

It was inspiring to meet men and woman who had killed Germans.

To fight among these brave men and woman, I would have walked for fourteen months. Now I would have my chance.

I was a partisan, a Jewish resistance fighter.

I had gone from ghetto to guerrilla.

# PARTISAN CAMP: LIVING IN THE FOREST

After two long weeks dodging the German army we had finally joined a partisan group consisting of about 250 dogged resistance fighters. It was a ragtag, yet effective outfit made up of mostly of Jewish men and some women from Baranowicze and numerous Russian officers, most of them prisoners of war who had escaped.

We were made to feel at home and instantly became part of this big, loose-knit group in the forest. They listened patiently to the story of our journey, then eagerly shared their own stories of escape, resistance, bravery and heroism.

Each tragic and heartfelt tale of personal suffering and grief was a battle unto itself; a small individual war that had been waged under incredible odds and won by sheer triumph of will and perseverance. Whether Russian POWs, Baranowicze Jews or the few local gentiles, the partisans we met on that first day – each and every one of them was a hero.

As I listened to their incredible stories by a roaring campfire, I wondered how my father would have felt if he could have seen me at this moment, the campfire flickering in my teary eyes, my body bruised and battered, but still intact after escaping and trudging two long weeks in the Polesie swamps and forest; the healthy glow on my ruddy face. I wondered what he would've thought seeing his son now.

---

And so our first few days as partisans began. Training started with background on our secluded location.

We learned that the Polish-Russian forest, in which we would fight our battles, was spread out over 1,000 miles. It signified a vast and ample hiding ground for the German troops and their deadly arsenal of weapons, tanks and artillery.

After careful consideration and much experimentation, the partisans had chosen the humid, muddy swamps as the main headquarters for our particular branch of operations. Despite the murky waters and muddy patches that served as makeshift moats around numerous dry islands, there was a healthy combination of sturdy trees and shrubs from which we gleaned enough wood to build our camps and stock our nightly campfires.

Like everything else in the partisan movement, the location had been chosen for safety reasons. For precautions and countermeasures, I soon learned that nothing in the forest was taken for granted, wasted, second-guessed or overlooked.

Every tree had its purpose, every branch a thousand uses particular to wartime. The towering trees and choking shrubs, the variety of foliage and thick vegetation made it easy for us to camouflage our meager stores of food, our meager cache of weapons and our smoldering fires.

The swamps were difficult to traverse. The Germans' lumbering cars, trucks and cumbersome cannons found the thick, wet mud and deep trenches of the forest virtually impassable; the swarms of mosquitoes, maddening.

Even with their extensive military expertise, it was hard for them to wage large-scale assaults, while the partisans, with their limited arsenal and wiry ways, were quite adept at fending off single attackers.

In the beginning we slept under the towering trees. Fallen needles were our mattresses, our dirty sleeves our pillows and shrubs and branches our covers.

Shortly after we arrived we were put to work making more suitable shelters for new partisans coming to the camp. These makeshift quarters looked like teepees with room for ten to sleep.

We built them on sparse dry patches of land, fitting between two-to-ten teepees in a group.

Like everything else that had to do with forest living in general – and partisan fighting in particular – our teetering teepees were designed for efficiency, whether putting them up, tearing them down or living in them.

We would build a fire in the center of each teepee, and men and women would sleep all around it: feet toward the fire to keep warm, heads radiating out like spokes of a wheel.

Just the simple act of starting a fire each night was challenging. With few supplies and even less technology, we went back to the Stone Age starting each and every fire by hand. Since it was such a long and tedious process, we tried to keep the fires burning twenty-four hours a day, only putting them out if we thought the Germans were coming. For former city dwellers it was a daunting and awkward task. But it was important to the cause and like everything else in life, I was determined to do it to the best of my ability.

No job was too minor, no task too menial. The gathering, the chopping, the building of the fire, and starting the fire were part of the process: a training program, an initiation.

In this way we got acclimated to the harsh realities of life in the rustic Polesie swamps. Dragging tree trunks through the forest, working side by side on the teepees, grunting over smoldering moss and flying sparks, we learned who we were living with, who we would be fighting with.

We ate more steadily, gained weight and rested more easily after long days of physical labor. Our muscles developed and our eyes adjusted to the pitch black of the forest nights. Even the soles of our city feet toughened. Gradually we were becoming true partisans.

Our training had begun. We learned how to guard our camp, how to stand watch and how to stay alert even when we were dead tired. We learned how to be over vigilant, how to patrol both in and around the camp, how to keep it safe and how to look for signs of German troops.

With the help of rugged partisan veterans, "old-timers" who were often under twenty-five themselves, we learned how to communicate with local farmers, peasants and villagers in the surrounding fields.

We found that some locals were sympathetic to the plight of the former Russian POWs and the Jewish people. Some despised Hitler, hated the Germans and what they had done to the Russian homelands. They were willing to risk their own safety and livelihoods.

Although they were actually part of our "training," these missions meeting the locals were neither simple nor risk-free. There was no such thing as a *sure* thing. No "easy" missions. In the dangerous world of the resistance movement, in the forest, in the field, nothing was ever guaranteed and even the smallest mission could go wrong – horribly wrong – in a thousand different ways.

But we had to try. We had to train as hard as we could, learn from our mistakes, anticipate the unforeseeable and avoid the unpreventable.

There were many different precautions that had to be taken before going on any mission. No one was allowed to go on a mission alone. No one. Not lieutenants, not captains, not veterans and especially not trainees. We always went in twos, threes or more, for our own safety and for the safety and security of the partisan movement itself.

After all, many of us were new to military operations, inexperienced in the art of war, although we had lived crushed beneath its violent tyranny.

We had few defenses and no discipline should we be captured.

There was no telling what a well-trained German soldier or even worse, an expert SS officer, could do to a hungry, dirty, tired, scared seventeen year-old.

Accordingly even the greenest partisan member always had a gun with him on an assignment. We were told to save one bullet no matter what, and the understanding behind the imperative was deadly clear. That last bullet was reserved for each of us, in case of capture. Better to kill ourselves than crack under torture and give up the location of the partisan camps or the names of any members.

We followed our leader, our fearless Russian partisan and crept when he crept, knelt when he knelt, slept when he slept. We took his lead, crouching at his signal, learning to communicate without speech through hand gestures or silent signs, the mute vocabulary of guerrillas.

While we younger partisans had limited knowledge in guerrilla warfare, we were quick learners, had courage and were fast runners.

Often my buddies and I walked for days to reach a new village, town or farm to contact a suspected sympathizer. As we had during our initial journey, we walked during the night and slept as best we could during the long, drawn-out day. I carried what I needed on my back – a little food, some water and extra bullets. Not much to fend off the well-outfitted and well-armed German army, but something.

---

After escaping from the ghetto and settling down in the partisans' camp, I had not bathed for two months, and neither had my comrades. We were all wearing the very same clothes we had escaped in. It was extremely cold and we had no facilities. My skin was brown and gray from sunburn and full of dirt and smoke from the campfire. I looked like a man from the Sahara Desert. I could not shave, so I cut my beard close to my skin with scissors. I almost never combed my hair. It was the same for most of us. On top of not being groomed and clean, my friends and I probably smelled like rotten cabbage. Imagine how we reeked after eating three or four heads of garlic with a piece of bread or a potato two or three times a day. But we did not notice it. Our noses became immune to this smell. Our bodies were immune to all conditions except death.

We always crept: around brush, behind trees, over barren fields and steep inclines, through farms and fields that cropped up in our path.

We never knew if there would be a German camp just over the horizon or a stealthy German soldier close on our backs. The houses and farms we visited could have held either friend or foe. We knocked on doors never knowing whether the man or woman on the other side would give us hot soup and warm bread or turn us in as soon as we left; never knowing if it would be our last fireplace or our last drink.

Fortunately we managed several missions without a hitch, encountering Jewish sympathizers we felt we could trust, gathering information for the cause, proving our worth and justifying our existence. Slowly, under the partisans' patient tutelage, we found volunteers who could be trusted to be our scouts, to serve as our spies – to provide intelligence about the German army's whereabouts and movements.

Our reach began to stretch beyond the secluded Polesie swamps, miles away, sometimes a long, cold, hungry walk of two nights or more. We found farmers, peasants and villagers who could tell us if German troops were passing through, where to find new partisan volunteers and the latest news and rumors from the front.

When we returned home from a mission, often three to four days after we had left, the camp was always the same. Sometimes there would be new faces, but for the most part it was familiar, stable and safe.

Despite the constant danger, despite the weariness and fear that it entailed, I preferred being out on a mission to sitting around camp.

---

Life in partisan camp was never easy, but soon a new menace cropped up that made it even more difficult. Incredibly, one of our worst problems was not fear, starvation, boredom or lack of sleep, it was something worse: lice.

We were totally infested with the pesky insects.

Ravenous and agile, they leapt from body to body, crawled from cap to scarf to sleeve to sock and spread like wildfire from the veterans to the new recruits and back again. Of all the pains and frustrations of ghetto life, we had been fortunate not to have to contend with these virulent, disease-bearing vermin.

Once you had them, it was almost impossible to get rid of them.

Our hygiene facilities were very poor. Aside from not having soap – oh what I would have given for one of my father's simple bars of soap – it was too cold to undress at night or to bathe in the morning and there was no place to wash clothes.

The partisans had a saying, "Do not undress, because in the morning your clothes will walk away." That is how bad the lice were. There were so many in our clothes, our shoes, our socks, that they could literally walk away with our wardrobe.

We suffered. The itching was terrible. No matter how tough you were, no matter how long you held out, no matter how much willpower you possessed, eventually you *had* to scratch. And once you started, you couldn't stop. It was the only relief from the itching, to scratch and scratch, risking infection from the open sores on your arms, neck, legs, belly – even your groin.

Eventually we contracted an epidemic of typhus from the lice. One hundred and five people got sick.

There was neither remedy for the infection nor cure for the epidemic. Those who were strong or young enough got over it. Many didn't. Dozens of partisans lost their toes or even part of a foot due to gangrene caused by poor circulation from the high fever. It was a miracle that nobody died from this plague, which lasted until October 1943.

When we were able to find an extra set of clothes, we would boil the lice-infested clothing we were wearing in a huge iron pot. From socks to underwear, from pants to shirts, it all went into the boiling water. We had to change every stitch of clothing in the freezing cold.

When we put our clothes above the fire and shook them, before dropping them into the boiling cauldron, we could actually see the lice falling off. We went through this ritual as often as we could.

We boiled and itched and we boiled some more. It was the only remedy. As the nights grew colder and colder, we picked up our camp and moved it deeper into the swamps.

Here we built bigger bunks from smuggled lumber and rough-hewn tree trunks 30 feet by 18 feet, designed to house up to 30 people at a time. In the middle of the bunk, we used a 50-gallon drum to make a roaring fire to keep us warm. Winters in this part of the country were notorious for being very cold and dumping huge amounts of thick, wet snow. The forest provided us with plenty of fuel and we tried to keep the fires burning all day long.

There were no beds inside the crude, ramshackle bunks. Instead, on each side along the length of the entire wall, we built one long shelf. There, curled up, everybody slept together, chin to chin, toe to toe – to keep warm and to stay safe. Even in cramped space on hard splintery wood, even with the snores and snorts and smells of thirty tired men and women, it was better than our beds back in the ghetto.

Here there was freedom instead of sudden and senseless death.

Here there were forests instead of fences.

Here in the forest and swamps that was our home, trees instead of Germans.

# MISHA AND THE MAKING OF A PARTISAN

We seldom got undressed, let alone bathed. We slept in our clothes, not just to keep warm, but for safety reasons. In case the Germans sneaked up on us, we would be able to run at a moment's notice. We had another saying: "The one who runs faster, lives longer."

Shortly after these new bunks were completed, a group of nearly 100 of us decided to split from the main camp, "Pugatchev's Brigade," to form our own company, which we called "Misha's *otriad,*" or Misha's group. We were still close to the old camp. A Russian captain by the name of Misha was our new commandant. Brave and strong, wise and experienced, Misha was soon to become much more than my leader. He would be my mentor, my hero and my guardian.

When I ran away from Baranowicze, I left my parents, my brother and my girlfriend Sima far, far behind. About a month after my escape, Sima was able to run away from the ghetto and join us in partisan camp. She came with her sister, her brother and her *new* boyfriend. Commandant Misha assigned them all to my bunk.

As you can imagine, I was very upset. Right away I told my girlfriend off for being unfaithful to me. All the anger, fire and hunger boiled over and found a target in her, with her young, delicate face. Here I was risking life and limb to become a partisan, joining the resistance and learning warfare and Sima was out cavorting with some other guy. She couldn't even wait a reasonable time before dating someone else?

It was a very uncomfortable situation those first few nights bunked up with my new arrivals, my old "friends." But I had more than my hurt pride on my mind.

Seeing my old girlfriend reopened old wounds that I had somehow been able to bury during the busy days of becoming a partisan. Seeing her made me miss my parents, my little brother, my home, my familiar bed. It made me miss my childhood and everything else that I had lost since the Germans invaded Baranowicze.

I missed my family.

A week after her arrival Sima dropped her boyfriend and found a new one, this time a Russian officer, a grown man who was also the commandant of a company in "Pugatchev's Brigade." A few weeks later they left to join another brigade someplace in the east closer to Minsk, someplace far away from me, my bunk and our camp.

I found out later from one of our scouts that they were killed by German soldiers in an ambush along the way. Fortunately her younger brother and sister had stayed behind with us.

Hearing this news about my former girlfriend, missing my family to the core and disillusioned by the hardships of life in partisan camp, I grew desperately homesick. Despite my bravado and the camaraderie of the other partisans, I began to notice how miserable the living conditions were.

The weather was bad and our hastily-built bunks, little more than shacks, hardly afforded shelter from the approaching winter storm.

All those dangerous, secret meetings with my cell back in the ghetto, all those childish dreams and macho visions of life as a partisan dissolved in the grim reality of day-to-day life. I grew sad and lonely, miserable and depressed. I was lost and alone: playing hard at being a grown-up and trying to become a strong, brave partisan.

I had been so tired, so hungry, so strong and so brave for so very long. Now I feared for the lives of my family and old friends.

What was once unthinkable, unimaginable and unforgivable became a very logical and sane decision: I decided to quit the partisans and return to the ghetto. I was ready to face death together with my family.

I was going to die, anyway, stranded out here starving to death on stolen cabbage roots, begging for vegetables, fighting fleas and lice and boredom instead of evil German soldiers. Why not die with my family? Why not die in my mother's arms? Why not give my little brother comfort in his last moments on earth?

I didn't want to live anymore. A blister grew on my heart; it festered, swelled and oozed until finally it popped. One day I looked around, stood up and simply started out.

No goodbyes, no souvenirs, no regrets.

No pack, no gun, no supplies.

But when I tried to leave the borders of the camp, when I dared to breach the perimeter, I was stopped by our guards. One of them went to Commandant Misha and told him I was trying to leave, that I had lost my mind.

Misha came out, walked over to me and without warning, without flinching, put a gun to my temple. In harsh language and without remorse, he ordered me to go back immediately or he would have no choice but to blow my head off. Literally, just like that, my life would be over.

A seventeen year-old failure.

I would be dead. Not by a German gun, not by a hangman's noose, not by starvation, but by the hand of my own commandant, my own captain, my own hero.

I had survived the German occupation of Baranowicze, weathered harsh German punishments and braved mean streets of the brutal ghetto. I had been spared at a dozen lineups, lived through two mass slaughters, risked life and limb to smuggle bullets past deadly guards, escaped at my own peril and wandered through the wilderness for two long weeks only to die senselessly at the hands of a Russian soldier who had vowed to train me, guide me and lead me.

I told Misha to go ahead and kill me, end my life, ease my suffering, I didn't care anymore. I was already dead anyway. Dead inside. My mind was numb; my heart had stopped beating days ago. Why not let my body catch up? He looked at me in disbelief, shock and horror. In *shame*. Then he took the gun away from my head and told me that too many Jews were being killed already, that too many innocent young lives had been lost, that he could not kill me.

Instead he slapped me on the shoulder, kicked me in the butt and ordered me back to camp with him. There Misha arranged for someone to give me a bath. Silently I wondered, Did he know I hadn't bathed for eight long weeks or did he instinctively realize it was just what I needed at that moment to snap me back to reality? It didn't matter. I didn't care. I reveled in my first bath since leaving the ghetto, watching the clean, hot water grow fizzy and fetid with over two months' worth of dirt, lice and grime.

After my bath Misha gave me fresh clothing, and plenty of food to eat. It was amazing what such simple, creature comforts did to revive my soul; how far I had come from the days as a schoolboy in Baranowicze when a hot bath and a good meal were taken for granted, along with clean clothes, my safety and most of all, my *freedom*.

After I was clean and dressed in new clothes, after I had eaten my fill, Misha talked to me for a very long time. I respected his experience and appreciated his sensitivity to my plight. He showed me kindness and I hung onto his every word.

He made me realize that dying would not help my family anymore than staying in the ghetto would have. He convinced me that my best hope was in committing my life to the partisan movement and doing my best to wreak havoc on the Germans.

This was my life now. This was the way to stay alive.

That day I became a real partisan warrior committed to helping destroy the German establishment. Where only hours ago I had been ready to end my life, now my life had a renewed purpose and I wanted to use it for the greater good. It was all due to Misha. He was a passionate individual, a runaway Russian officer and former POW who had seen and done things I could only dream about.

Apparently Misha was as impressed with me as I was with him. A few weeks after our talk, he divided our group of 98 partisans into 3 separate units, each comprised of 31 men, 1 company commandant and 4 people in the kitchen.

To my surprise he had the trust to put me in command of one of these divisions, the second company, unit #2. When I asked him why, he told me that I was a responsible young man and that I had the personality, the courage and the character of a born leader.

Most of the men assigned to my command were about my age and some had been in school with me.

I was determined to lead them as best I could.

I was determined not to let Misha or my family or myself down again.

I was determined to do my best for my unit, for my country, for Misha and for myself.

I was ready to fight for my people, to make a difference, to be a part of the partisan movement with all of my heart and soul, all of my spirit and blood and all of my sweat and tears.

I was ready to fight and *kill* Germans.

# WOODEN GUNS AND FOOD MISSIONS

*Winter 1942*

Events in the world outside were slowly building. News of Hitler's secret death camps, of his claustrophobic ghettos, of his brutal torture, of his unlimited madness, had finally reached the newspapers – from Washington to London, from Denmark to Moscow.

Sometimes the chilling stories were even accompanied by gruesome photographs, stolen snapshots from death camps at Auschwitz, Buchenwald and Bergen-Belsen.

Finally the British, Russian and American allies were gathering strength, gearing up for the fight, mounting massive deployments of troops. But despite their military might and their determination, it would still be months, even years, before engagement.

In the meantime the dogged partisans bravely soldiered on. The Germans were still out there, murdering our families. No one could help us but ourselves.

Life in our partisan camp was as harsh as ever. Maybe even more so.

In the beginning, the food in camp had been barely edible. We had survived on little more than potatoes, flour, a little bit of lard, a few onions and the occasional dash of coarse, peasant salt. The women took care of the makeshift kitchen. From such meager ingredients they managed to cook soup for all of us. Soup for breakfast, lunch and dinner.

We understood the necessity for such a frugal dish, and soup was the most efficient way to stretch our limited food supplies. It also provided us with much-needed warmth for our bodies and our souls.

Most of the food we gathered to fill the gurgling kettles of thin "partisan soup" was supplied by the same farmers and villagers upon whom we relied for information, support and, occasionally, inspiration.

These brave citizens wholly supported the partisan movement and were as vital to our cause as the veteran Russian officers who trained us. These hearty peasants hated the Germans with a passion and saw Hitler as "a human incarnation of the Devil."

For a while the system worked. Three or four of us would go on a local "food mission," venturing out into the nearby forests looking for friendly farmers and villagers.

We would take what meager rations of food they could spare, ever mindful that these peasants had to feed their own families as well.

As the surrounding ghettos were slowly liquidated and the daily terror grew worse, more Jewish souls fled to our camp. The already anemic stores of food started running out.

It was a simple if unavoidable equation. If we were hungry at our present head count, we would soon be starving if the numbers of Jews continued to mount. New recruits meant more manpower, for building, for gathering, for fighting, for sabotage, but also more mouths to feed. More water in the soup. More bowls to pass around in camp.

We had to find a way to feed everyone. To accommodate our growing numbers, our fearless commandant decided to send some of us beyond our normal "comfort zone," beyond our predictable range of Jewish sympathizers and "friendlies."

Misha started to send us farther out to find food, to distant villages that were a long way from our base camp.

Some times we would walk for 2 or 3 nights just to reach a village, spend a night scoping it out before approaching it, then another 2 or 3 nights of walking to return. A week's hard travel for extra bags of potatoes, flour, loaves of bread and a pocket's worth of salt to keep our camp members fed.

These missions grew more dangerous as time wore on. These distant villagers really did not want to help us. They were German sympathizers, but grudgingly handed over potatoes, flour and lard.

After a few brief missions, however, we realized that their resistance was much too strong. To scare them into handing over some of their food, we used fake guns made out of wood.

At this point in the war effort we still hadn't gathered guns from the local citizenry.

There were a handful of weapons in camp, mostly Russian rifles and pistols, but not nearly enough to arm the whole camp. Our weapons cache was so low that we could only afford to let one partisan carry a gun on each mission.

Some times we left the safety of our base camp with nothing more than a 1 grenade between the 3 or 4 of us. This was barely enough to fend off an attacker or intimidate a stubborn villager.

And so, for a time, we relied solely on these fake wooden guns to bluff our way.

We had to take chances because we needed to eat and, at this time, this was the only way to find food. We were risking our lives to stay alive. There was no lack of trees in the forest to fell for these crude, imitation guns. We spent countless hours whittling them into nearly exact replicas of the Russian weaponry we had on hand as models.

As I whittled in the frosty winter air, the acrid smell of the campfire and the bitter cold in my bare fingers all seemed to drift away as I recalled the lost and carefree days of my innocent childhood. So far away, so long ago…

My family had been poor but resourceful. Penniless but proud. As a result, both of my nurturing parents had taught my brother and me to be creative and resourceful when it came to entertaining ourselves. Despite my father's high degree of formal education and his professional background as an accountant, his status as a Jew in Poland (the Poles did not like the Jews) during the time of growing Nazi oppression deprived him of work.

I remember one year it seemed as if everyone on the block was getting new scooters for birthday presents.

I was determined to build a scooter for my brother and myself. I noticed a new construction site in our neighborhood. Piled near the rusty, overflowing rubbish bins was a large stack of cast-off lumber. After school one day I brazenly walked directly onto the hectic lot and asked for the foreman.

Bemused, the foreman barely flinched when I asked him if I could have some of the discarded wood. "Take all you can carry," he answered with a grin.

I did.

There was other debris in the trash heap as well. Old ball bearings and bent nails, dented cans half full of paint and lacquer. I availed myself of these priceless items as well. Back home in the backyard, I fashioned my own scooter from scrap lumber and bent nails. With an observant eye, I copied the lines and mechanisms of the other kids' scooters. Before long, my little brother and I were taking turns scooting up and down the block on our very own homemade scooter.

No one could believe it had been made by hand. They all said it looked like it came straight out of a store. They all seemed so surprised. But I wasn't. I had seen something I wanted. I had seen a way to make it for myself. And I had done it. I was eleven at the time.

Now I wanted something very different from the childhood scooter. I wanted more food for a camp full of hungry, Jewish partisans. Instead of a homemade scooter, I was chopping down trees and making fake guns. We used black and silver lacquer to adorn the unfinished wood and painted the guns to look as real as possible. They looked very believable under the cover of a dark and frosty night.

Misha, who had also been going on these dangerous but vital missions, reminded us of just how crucial they were. I never experienced the slightest pang of guilt threatening these farmers. The fear in their eyes as I tried to make my fake gun look heavy and leaden never bothered me. These were not friendly farmers. These were not the brave peasants of our local villages who had always helped us with information and support.

I never forgot for a second that these people cowering in front of me were Nazi sympathizers aiding German soldiers to capture, torture and kill Jews and partisans. The distant villages in which they lived, the farms on which they toiled, were controlled by the German army.

---

Another problem we faced was snow. At first we could not walk in freshly fallen snow for fear of leaving tell-tale footprints that would lead the Germans straight to our camp.

We devised a way to conquer this dilemma. One man would lead while the rest of us streamed behind. Carefully – literally – we followed in our leader's footsteps. Luckily we only had to do that until we reached the road, which was about a half a mile away.

The second man in line would then very carefully step into the footprints of the first, and the third man would walk just as cautiously into the footprints of the second, and so on, until it looked as if only one man was walking. It was much easier for the falling snow to cover one set of footprints than the wide swath of foot prints we spread. We also began wearing long white coats on top of our clothes so that we blended in with the white wintry forest.

Before the winter turned deadly cold that first season in the forest, before the snow began to fall and imprint our footprints, we could still make use of the horses and buggies on loan from our friendly farmers and villagers.

As my buddies and I traveled into distant territories, we would lead the horse along, the rattletrap buggy teetering onward and upward behind us. We learned that once a horse knew the path there, he would return home alone, if need be. Such was this animal's intelligence that it could find its way back after traveling the route only once.

And so, on our return, we would let the horse lead the way. Falling behind, we would walk warily behind the buggy, staying close to the trees and shrubs thickly lining both sides of the crude footpath, ever watchful for German soldiers hiding in the brush waiting to ambush us.

Opening fire on the innocent horse instead of on us, the German soldiers would give away their position, allowing us to escape into the woods.

It was another trick, another guerrilla survival tactic.

---

One night after traveling several days to a distant village, the villagers refused to give us food. Our scraggly raiding party of 3 scruffy partisans and our phony wooden guns failed to work their usual magic.

Not only did these villagers refuse to hand over the food we demanded, they even threatened to report us to the Germans.

With ice-cold fear in our pounding hearts, we threatened to come back and kill them if they gave us away.

We headed back to camp. After we conferred with Misha, we decided to use a larger squad, one made up of 11 men.

Returning to the same village with the additional men to back us up, not to mention real guns mixed in with the toy ones, the villagers soon got the message.

Frightened into submission, they agreed to give us potatoes, flour, cabbage heads and lard.

But who could tell what they would do with their growing anger?

Soon it appeared that these distant villagers had made good on their word to inform the Nazis. We started spotting an unprecedented number of new German soldiers in these sensitive areas.

Now it became too dangerous to go. What had once been just a "dangerous" assignment to secure food had suddenly become a suicide mission.

# MAKING MORE NOISE

With local farmers and country peasants barely surviving on their own, dwindling stores of food and distant villages all but controlled by the ever-present Germans, our food missions almost ground to a disappointing halt.

Soon we were encountering serious problems with our vanishing food supply. Though we watched our pantry carefully, our daily rations of soup grew smaller and smaller, with fewer servings to more people every day; the soup itself, thinner and thinner.

During this bleak and hungry time we learned how to make flour from grain, grinding it between two round, flat stones until it was as fine as possible. Cooked in water and boiled to a gelatinous consistency that was far worse than gruel, we lived on this homemade flour. We had no salt, no fat, no meat for flavoring. It was like eating glue. We had this miserable meal three times a day: glue for breakfast, glue for lunch and glue for dinner. This horrid concoction was indigestible, but our bodies adjusted, sucking out what little nutrients it contained to keep us going. We persevered stomach cramps, bowel obstructions and constipation.

To prepare for the dead of winter, Misha assigned us to build more bunks. We used the thin birch trees that populated the thick surrounding forests. They were the perfect building material because they always grew straight up and despite their size could withstand pounds of pressure before snapping in two.

We dug the new bunks three-to-four feet deep into the ground. Next we covered them with rows and rows of the resilient birch logs for a makeshift roof. Finally we covered the log roofs with a protective mixture of straw, sand, branches and leaves so that the bunks would blend in with the surrounding scenery.

We built five separate bunks for our living quarters, a separate kitchen bunk and a storage bunk that included a primitive kind of bath.

About two hundred feet from where we dug the bunks, we built two bathrooms, one for the women and one for the men. We used the same basic structure as the living bunks, crafting them half as large. We camouflaged them for privacy as well as security. These restrooms were really little more than big holes in the ground dug five feet deep.

Although it was a camp, an open area vulnerable to the elements, it was where we lived day in and day out. We not only had to keep it camouflaged for safety reasons but also for sanitary reasons as well. We were already going through a deadly bout of typhus fever from the massive lice infestation and had to avoid dysentery and other diseases that resulted from human waste that had not been disposed of properly.

Located about five miles from the village of Swiatica, we stayed in this "bunker camp" for the entire winter of 1942 and spring of 1943. This was our home base from where all our missions originated.

The severe and brutal conditions that existed were extremely difficult. Local farmers from Swiatica and Zaluze helped out. Without them, the partisan movement may not have been possible and may not have survived.

In order to carry out our clandestine activities, the farmers used to guide us through the thick forest and lead us in the right direction.

They assisted with building our camp and guided us to different places for the resources we needed. These farmers also helped us find old rifles, grenades and ammunition left over from the Russian military.

The members of my company were steadily becoming a better and stronger fighting group, relying more on each other, instinctively communicating in the dead of night without speaking, following each other's lead.

However our communication with the main partisan leadership was slow because we did not have equipment for the proper relaying of messages, not even telephones or radios. Everything was done through human contact, at night and on foot.

We were seeking armaments for more dangerous missions. Some local villages dredged up a few old guns, rifles, grenades and other useful explosives. They might have been out of date and dusty, but these secondhand weapons enabled us to step up our sabotage efforts. Holding a weapon in my hands, feeling the cold steel, was comforting. Tromping back in the falling snow, lugging our booty on our shoulders, we returned triumphant, our successful efforts adding significantly to our growing cache of weapons.

It felt good to deliver weapons into the hands of a smiling Misha, who would slap me on the back proudly, roughly, and in Russian, tell me "Good job" or "Well done, brother."

We began to "make more noise," as we called it in those heady days of daily heroics. We began creating confusion, causing disruptions and generally disturbing the Germans' peace, throwing weekly monkey wrenches into the great, heaving cogs of machinery that was the mighty German war machine. We made it harder for them to operate efficiently, hit them where it hurt and where they least expected it. We started using various explosives like grenades and Molotov cocktails – vodka or beer bottles filled with kerosene and a cloth "wick" – to destroy small businesses and shops that supplied various merchandise to the German military.

After the rush of a successful mission, despite the heroics, the tactics and the resourcefulness, I always felt a painful twinge of sorrow that the only place where my family might still be alive was in my imagination. And when I dredged them up to find the courage to take action against the Germans, I was haunted by the pale faces of my mother, my father and my little brother.

Shopkeepers – butchers, and tailors and jewelers – were not our only targets. On a few missions my buddies and I destroyed small bridges to disrupt the movement of the German army's trucks, trucks that brought supplies to the very same German soldiers who were hunting us. Many routes became impassable due to our efforts, leaving the German army stranded by the roadside for days on end.

Where there was no bridge to blow up, no river for the German army to cross, we disrupted the movements of their trucks by blocking well-traveled roads and trails with heavy logs and boulders from the nearby forest, occasionally killing a few German soldiers in the process. Anything we could do to slow down or damage the German war effort was worth the risk. Delaying army trucks, even by a day, might mean the difference. Delaying a shipment of uniforms, sturdy boots, winter clothing, weapons or ammunition to the front line, might mean the difference between German success – or defeat.

These trucks also carried hundreds of men to the Russian front. Slowing the delivery of these soldiers by even one day or one hour could mean triumph for the Russian army and its allies.

We were scrawny Jews, seventeen, eighteen and nineteen

years old. Escapees. Refugees. We were fighting back. We were risking everything to make a difference one day at a time. We were spitting in Hitler's face.

Up to now we had suffered very few casualties on our nighttime raids.

However it wasn't always possible to outrun the enemy. One of my men was killed during an unfortunate ambush, another seriously wounded on a separate occasion.

For the amount of damage we were doing, the delays we were causing and the risks we were taking, the odds had been decidedly in our favor.

The German response to our successful clandestine missions was a concerted campaign to find the partisans, to hunt down the freedom fighters in our area and to finish us off for good.

It was the German army's intent to cleanse the forest of all the partisans, all the guerrillas, just like they were ridding nearby towns, hamlets and villages of all the Jews.

For days they searched the forests.

The pristine, virgin white snow of the rustic landscape soon grew black with gunpowder and soot. The forest trees shook with mortar rounds, their branches exploding into a thousand pieces, their splinters littering the dirty snow.

The grim specter of violence had moved deep into our forest.

Suddenly, for the first time, we heard warning shots – three successive rifle blasts – from our perimeter guards at the farthest outpost, three miles from camp.

The German military was moving in the direction of our two partisan camps in the middle of the forest.

Misha immediately issued an order for everyone to leave the camp and start running in the opposite direction of the warning shots. There were about 250 partisans, men, women and a few children. We all began to scatter.

In Misha's group, there was a mother who had three children

between the ages of three and seven. Their father was on a mission with some other men. To run faster, we decided that we would take turns carrying one of the children for fifteen minutes at a time and then transfer them to another partisan to carry for the next fifteen minutes. This worked for awhile – until the children started to cry. No matter what anyone tried to do, there was no one in the group of almost 100 who could stop the children from crying. Instead, they began to cry even more loudly, putting us all in a life-threatening situation.

In the dry, cold winter in the forest, voices traveled quite a distance. Any noise could be heard far away. Either the crying children had to be quieted or we would all die. We stopped running to find a solution.

Captain Misha proposed that the mother and her children stay behind in a field and hide in a haystack. They would be given enough food for a week. Misha would also give the mother his sheep pelt vest to keep her children warm and his own revolver. We all swore to her that we would return as soon as it was clear, in one or two days. Misha said that if none of us returned, she was to assume we had been killed.

But this woman stubbornly refused to accept Misha's offer and the children's crying kept getting louder and louder! Any moment now, they would give away our position.

Everyone pleaded with the mother to accept the offer, to trust us as this was a matter of life or death for all of us. The crying of the children was creating panic within the group.

Misha conferred with all of us and then announced that since it was his responsibility to protect the lives of 250 partisans, if the mother refused to cooperate he had no other choice but to shoot the children. One lady even offered to stay back with them, and still the mother refused that. Again Misha pleaded with her to no avail. That mother would not budge. She told Misha in front of everybody to kill her children; she wasn't going to stay with them in the haystack.

Throughout this ordeal that mother never blinked an eye, never wavered. Kill her own children! It was beyond belief.

Everyone began to cry – "Kill the children, our sweet Jewish children!"

It was bad enough for the Germans to do it, but for us? It was just too much to bear.

With tears in his eyes Misha gave the mother one last chance, asking her to please accept the offer. When she refused again, Misha, with a trembling hand, shot the three children through his pelt vest and then cried.

A group of men put the bodies of the children together, covered them with the pelt, and put forest branches on top of them to hide the bodies from the Germans.

There was not a dry eye in the entire camp. Many were praying.

Then we turned around and ran faster and faster into the forest. The will to survive was stronger than our anguish.

We had almost been annihilated, but under Misha's leadership we survived.

Two days later we returned to the makeshift burial ground and tenderly gathered the children's bodies, brought them back to camp and gave them a proper burial.

---

The farmers had informed us that there had been over 1,000 German soldiers searching the forest for us. For all their expert training, for all their modern weaponry, their superior numbers and firepower, their mighty intelligence and their planning, the Germans lacked the ability that the Russians, whom they had already beaten, and the Jews, whom they could so easily exterminate, had: to be able to live deep and secluded in the forest by managing to control themselves and their surroundings.

What army could ever hope to match a hungry band of renegade teenagers, almost all of them orphaned and all of them intent on carrying out swift and bloody revenge for the murders of their schoolmates, teachers, neighbors, friends and families?

Now that the Germans knew where we had been, Misha decided to split the group into 3 smaller units and relocate. Two of the groups traveled east out of the forest in the direction of Minsk, but Misha's group, which was still made up of escapees from the Baranowicze ghetto, remained.

While I feared the German army's return, I was determined to stay as close to Baranowicze as was possible. Who knew when my family would escape or when I would be able to rescue them? As the other groups prepared to leave, my resolve to stay was unshaken. My former cell mates from the ghetto agreed. Our group of 98 settled deep in the forest, about fifty-five miles south of Baranowicze, and quickly grew to 138 full-time partisans.

Again Misha divided us into four squads of 31 fighters each, in addition to a group composed of one commandant and 13 partisans, who attended to camp chores on a revolving basis.

I was the leader of the second squad. It felt good to be considered a "veteran." Though my family never left my mind for an instant, there were times when my partisan activities almost erased the painful memories of them back in the ghetto; when Baranowicze seemed a million miles and a thousand years away, when the ghetto seemed a figment of my imagination.

Our primary mission remained two-fold: first, to inflict on the Germans as much discomfort and damage as possible and, second, to help the Russians and their allies destroy the German war machine.

The German army never accomplished its goal in the forest. They never found us. And one day the machine-gun fire and the grenades just stopped. As suddenly as it began, the German's massive "search and destroy" mission was over. They hadn't found a thing. The Germans gave up and left.

---

A few days before Christmas 1942 I had a very big surprise – one that stirred up all the fears that had haunted me since I left my family behind in the ghetto. Out of nowhere, my cousin, Abraham Portnow, appeared. He told us the amazing story of his escape and survival and of the tragic loss of another relative.

There had been 4 of them: Abraham, his girlfriend, his brother Israel and another Jewish girl. Unlike my escape, which had gone unnoticed by the enemy, on the second day of their departure they were spotted by German soldiers, detected trying to cross a flat, barren, two-hundred-foot expanse of open field between one side of the neighboring forest and the other. In that instant, in that postage stamp of land between freedom and safety, between life and death, the German soldiers and the Belarus policemen ambushed them mercilessly from behind a line of trees.

They all ran, but Abraham's brother and the two Jewish girls were instantly killed in a spray of machine-gun fire.

Poor Abraham, after seeing what had happened to his girlfriend, his brother and the other girl, had somehow managed to escape, fleeing on foot through the countryside until he found our camp and refuge.

A week after my grieving cousin Abraham had arrived with his tragic tale, a strange man in rags showed up on the outskirts of our camp, claiming that he was my cousin Israel, Abraham's brother. Abraham's *dead* brother? How could that be?

The scruffy, starving stranger claiming to be my cousin also was blond with startling blue eyes and the guards on duty that day were suspicious that this person, claiming to be Israel, was really a German spy trying to infiltrate our camp. They could have killed him, but instead they brought him into the camp so that I might confirm whether or not he was, in fact, my cousin; so that poor Abraham might confront the man impersonating his dead brother!

As the suspected traitor stood in front of us, Abraham and I thought we were looking at a ghost. Dressed in rags and shivering, the answer to a lost prayer, it *was* Abraham's brother, my cousin Israel! We rushed to embrace him. There were hugs, tears, questions, then new clothes and a hot meal for the newcomer.

Misha welcomed Israel warmly, knowing that his presence was proof that miracles did exist. Israel's story confirmed for us the age-old adage that the truth is, indeed, stranger than fiction.

When the Germans were shooting at Abraham, Israel and the two Jewish girls, bullets whizzing past their heads, Israel stumbled and fell to the ground. His heart pounding, his face buried in damp soil, his body trembling from fear and panic, on instinct he pretended to be dead.

Holding his breath, clamping his eyes shut, he willed his body to stop shivering against the cold, barren ground. He stayed absolutely still as the German soldiers approached him, rifles pointed at his back. He could not tell how many of them there were or what they were doing as they surrounded him, cursing in German, poking him, prodding him and searching through his pockets.

They even undressed him, not realizing he was alive, and left him for dead, face down in the snow. There he lay, naked, freezing and all alone. He heard the Germans laughing, talking and smoking as if they had merely relieved themselves while on break.

As Abraham was running away, he turned around and thought he saw the policeman shoot Israel in the head. But that shot had missed. In fact Israel believed the policeman had missed on purpose, even though he knew he was a Jew fleeing the Baranowicze ghetto to freedom.

After he was sure that they were gone, Israel stood up and ran, ran for his life, in grief and in shame; naked, bewildered and frightened.

Israel told us that he had stopped at the first house he found in the nearest hamlet and begged its occupants for something, anything, to cover his freezing, naked body. They gave him what they could: a few old, ill-fitting rags, worn-out shoes that didn't fit and some potato sacks to keep his body warm at night, what he was still wearing when he showed up. They also gave him directions to the nearest partisan camp.

It took him six days and nights in frozen conditions without food to find us.

Abraham and I could not understand how Israel did not freeze to death during the first few hours because temperatures during the past week had been well-below zero.

Whatever the reason, there Israel was standing in front of us, alive, with no fingers or toes lost to frostbite.

For this, we were eternally grateful. For this, we would ignore all the mysteries of the universe and simply be content with the outcome.

# THE FINAL SLAUGHTER

*Christmas 1942*

In the weeks before Christmas refugees from the ghetto flooded the campsite.

That was how I learned who died, of the deaths of my wonderful, loving Aunt Rosa and my cousins, Lutek, Frieda, Minar, Genia and Simar. I was very depressed.

Then, in hushed tones and halting speech, a cell mate who had wearily found his way to our secluded camp, told me that an old friend of mine from school, a young teenager called Jankele had died. But he hadn't just died. He had been killed by the Germans, aimed at for target practice and used as an example for the entire ghetto to see.

It turns out that Jankele and 2 friends, other young schoolmates of mine, had sensed a change in the air. Following their instincts, they tried to escape.

The bereft man with panic in his eyes, his hands trembling, struggled to find the right words. While trying to run from the ghetto, while frantically attempting to scale that dreaded, barbed wire fence, the three boys were caught by the ruthless German soldiers on patrol and shot to death.

But instead of taking these 3 boys, these 3 children, down off the fence so their families could give them a proper funeral and bury them with the respect they deserved, the Germans left them hanging right where they had been shot, dangling from the barbed wire; human scarecrows on display, limbs akimbo – facing the fields of freedom they tried to reach.

Their parents were forced to pass by their children each day and night on the way to and from work. Their boyhood chums, girlfriends, neighbors, shopkeepers and former teachers casting their eyes down the street as they passed, yet unable to avoid the unforgettable sight and the stench of their decaying bodies.

For one solid week, seven long, agonizing days, those boys were left hanging on that fence before being taken down and discarded.

---

The stories of those lucky to have escaped were chilling; their voices choked, their eyes haunted. We questioned them about our families in an attempt to shed light on what had happened to those we left behind. And, slowly, we were able to piece together the details, the facts of what took place in the *third* and final slaughter on Christmas Day 1942.

The soldiers had come in the morning, knocking down doors, crashing in windows, beating entire families, driving them from their ghetto homes in their bedclothes, dragging them like dogs into the city streets.

My remaining family members had survived the *third* slaughter, but they were finally separated from each other, even my mother and father, who had not been apart for a single night their entire marriage!

My father was sent to Koldychevo, a small labor camp holding 127 Jewish men and a few women. The inmates were tailors, dressmakers, shoemakers, jewelers, barbers and chemists, the "professional tradesman," as the Germans called them. But while my heart was broken that my father had been separated from his family, I was encouraged because his camp was not far from Baranowicze. We were only about sixty miles from Koldychevo, a mere three-day hike for a pack of young partisans bent on rescue. My sincere hope was to liberate my father and bring him to our camp.

And though I was glad to hear that my mother and my little brother were, in fact, still alive, I was less confident that they could be saved.

A lady who came to partisan camp told me that my mother and my brother, at the first sounds of gunfire, at the first signs of slaughter, immediately took refuge in a cramped L-shaped bunker beneath somebody's house, where they were joined by other family members, friends and neighbors. They clung together in silence, dreading the footsteps that would come, the search that would follow and the deadly bullets that would rain down on them from above. For, by now, the Germans were wise to the ways of the ghetto dwellers.

Aided by gentile sympathizers who would sell a human soul for the price of a pack of cigarettes, German soldiers found the bunker. Showing no mercy, the Germans went in with machine guns and sprayed the occupants of the bunker below like they were shooting fish in a barrel.

But the German soldiers only sprayed the long part of the bunker's L shape. Crouched in the short space that made up the rest of the L were my mother, my brother and two other lucky Jews who had escaped the hail of gunfire, squeezing further and further into the earthen walls as the bloody violence erupted beside them.

Hearing nothing but the sound of their own labored breathing and the dripping of innocent blood, the German soldiers, thinking their job complete, left; the 4 survivors below clinging to each other in disbelief; in mourning.

After two days without food or water and unable to stand the stench of the gore any longer, they decided to leave the bunker and seek other shelter. With little to lose, they ran to a nearby brick factory, where, amazingly, other survivors had congregated.

In the days that followed, though, the Germans found the brick factory as well. But instead of killing the Jews right off they put them to work for the war effort, making bricks and building supplies for the insatiable German military machine.

Only 235 Jews survived the final slaughter that deadly Christmas day. Those 235 Jews, including my mother and my little brother, were the last of the 13,000 peaceful Jews who lived ordinary lives in and around Baranowicze and were massacred in the ghetto.

The Germans had slaughtered 13,000 Jews like dirty swine.

And 13,000 Jews were gone forever.

None of us could ever forget the *first* slaughter on Purim 1942. Some of us still went to bed each night hearing the cries of our families. We all died a little when we saw our friends carted away in trucks, clawing at the doors, screaming for their lives. We had heard the shrill alarm at 8 a.m., then saw the elegant yellow gloves and the pink fingers flicking right and left. The horror of the blonde pregnant officer's wife demonically killing our little ones.

Rosh Hashanah 1942, another massacre: 21 of us, naked and sweating in our clandestine bunker, drenched in misery, horror and fear.

As I sat reviewing the events since the start of the war, I pulled my father's coat tighter around me – my father's only coat. The coat I took from him the night I left the ghetto to join a new family, to go down a different path.

As I pledged allegiance to my fellow partisans, I had followed them far, far away from the man who had raised me, from the mother who had held me, from the little brother who looked up to me. My father's coat was a bittersweet reminder of the decision I had made: the life I had chosen, the family I had left behind.

# GUERRILLA WARFARE

*Spring 1943*

Spring finally came to our secluded base camp, though you couldn't always tell by the weather. As January turned to February, then to March and winter slowly loosened its knotty grip on the Lipiczany Forest, nights were still bitter, days little better and the sun only occasionally poking through thick, white snow clouds. Deep inside the forest, where the tall pine, oak and birch trees nearly blotted out the sun and gave us shelter from our enemies, it was also a good ten degrees colder than outside the forest.

Despite constant danger, there were the occasional tender, almost beautiful moments, which brought laughter to our grim, bleak faces and, occasionally, tears to our eyes.

We were on a mission to burn down a German officer's house. On the way there 3 of us took a shortcut, walking beside the bank of a nearby river. There had been a wild snowstorm that week that left a sleek sheet of frozen ice. That day was heart-stopping cold and windy, though the storm had abated.

We had nothing but trouble walking through the blustery conditions, slipping on exposed sheets of crackling white ice, grabbing hold of each other or clinging to the relative safety of a nearby tree to keep ourselves from eating a face full of snow – or perhaps even falling and breaking an arm or leg.

Walking alongside the partially frozen river might not have been the safest route that day, but it would save us about eight miles in freezing conditions. Eight long miles of running noses and frozen toes. A few slips here, a little hazard there, was well worth the gain.

As we were carefully wending our way along the slippery riverbank, making slow headway, one man fell on an errant patch of ice, landing flat on his face, his arms and legs sprawling.

As my partner and I stooped down to help him, the frigid winter wind picked him right up and blew him far from our reach, dragging him across the slippery bank of creaking river ice. The wind was so strong, the breeze so swift, that it sped him straight toward the middle of the river where the water was rushing with the springtime melt.

Despite below-freezing temperatures in the depths of the forest, often hovering at sub-zero degrees, the flowing river water was always moving. Constantly in motion, day and night, it never froze. Even the ice beneath our partner's slip-sliding rump was perilously thin, threatening to crack wide open at any moment. Trying not to panic, racing to help, we knew that we had to reach him before he hit the rapidly flowing water.

Luckily we found a long tree branch on the ground. Lying down on the tenuous riverbank myself, I reached forward with the branch while my partner held onto my boots for dear life. I could feel his vise-like grip through the worn leather as I strained for all I was worth to make myself just that much longer.

We were able to push the branch to our partner's reach, and he scrambled like mad until his blue and aching frozen fingers finally found purchase among the twigs and leaves we'd extended. He grabbed the branch with all his might, a look of relief filling his face, and clung on for dear life. Awkwardly, slowly, we pulled our friend back to the riverbank. When he was safe, when the ice beneath his frozen body no longer creaked, we dropped the branch and raced to drag him up onto his knees, shaking like a newborn colt. We had saved his life.

We hugged as brothers. In this embrace, I felt his body trembling and knew it wasn't from the snow or the cold. Tears of gratitude were frozen on his rosy cheeks. After our fright subsided we talked and joked about this near catastrophe with an easy laugh and a feeling of gratitude.

We went on and carried out our mission.

I remember that rescue as one of the few happy experiences we had during our bleak and frantic lives.

---

Unfortunately life and death struggles in the deep, dark forest didn't always end so happily.

Each and every mission was considered a "deadly" one, whether anyone was actually injured or not. The possibility of danger, the fear of ambush, the element of surprise, of betrayal, of persecution, was always present on every mission. Few of the actual missions took more than a few minutes to accomplish. We got in, did what we had to do, got out and that was that. Our missions were silent, efficient and, most of all, effective.

Even the traveling was not so bad. Though it often took days on end – traipsing through the forest, winding through the trees, becoming one with the deep, dark night, slipping in under the seamless cover of night, creeping silently through thick and dense black forests, navigating around the narrow borders of towns and villages, skirting ambushes and taking no foolish risks – we usually arrived at our destination unscathed.

The most dangerous part of a mission was not the actual mission itself. No, it was always the traveling – the to and from, the coming and going – that was the dangerous part of the mission, especially the return.

For, after completing a mission, many of which resulted in an explosion, a major loss of property or a burning building lighting up the night sky like a fireworks display, it was difficult to simply slink back into the night unnoticed and disappear without a trace.

Many times the German army, alerted by a watchful guard or a local member of their intricate and far-reaching network of collaborators and spies, followed closely behind us. Some times they surprised us with troops, lying in wait along our path, machineguns at the ready to ambush us.

At such times we had a hard and fast rule: when fleeing from engagement with the enemy always split into three separate directions. Whether there were five of us on a mission, or fifteen, we never wavered from this rule.

A group of us would run straight, another would tear off along a second path and the rest would veer off in a third direction. It was an ingenious partisan tactic, a lesson straight from the ever-expanding guerrilla playbook; a deadly game of odds. In one direction might bring life; in another, death.

Invariably the German forces stuck together as a team, an elite unit thinking, acting and running as one, pursuing only one of our groups until machine-gun fire signaled a chilling climax. Or, as would happen in many cases, frustrated German troops coming up short again.

We all understood that the life of a partisan was one of severe odds and high stakes. Sooner or later our luck could run out as well. All we could hope for was that it would happen later rather than sooner!

The longer we survived, the better we handled our escapes, the more we could do for the cause and for our people.

The area in which we conducted on our clandestine missions was as far as one could get from the easily-navigated streets of Baranowicze.

The fields, forests and swamps where we lived, slept, worked and killed covered almost two hundred miles in diameter along what was once the Polish-Russian border. To those of us who had grown up in apartments, treading stairs to get to the front door and weaving in and out of city streets on scooters, the distance was unimaginable. To those of us who had to travel its borders and penetrate its darkness, it was bigger still.

On more than one occasion I had been part of a mission that found itself stuck and floundering in the dead of night, desperately lost and helpless, bumping into trees and shrubs, tripping over roots and vines because we could not see our hands in front of our faces. More than once we were rescued by a farmer who had grown up in these stark, silent woods and could navigate them blindfolded. The farmers in the nearby villages of Swiatica and Zaluze continued to be a constant and unwavering source of support.

They were somewhat repaid by the safety our presence afforded them and, for the most part, lived quietly, their villages and farms hardly touched by the death and destruction around them. Because the Germans could not invest in the manpower to hunt us down, these locals were also left alone.

Wyganoszcze was a small, charming hamlet of about 800 people living and working on the border of our territory; good people, loyal sympathizers.

We were on a mission just beyond there when the unmistakable sound of violence and brutality drew us to its borders.

A well-organized squad of German soldiers had rounded up everyone in the village. Almost the entire population of this little hamlet milled around nervously on the grounds of a church; several German trucks parked nearby, engines running.

About one hundred yards from where we stood, senseless acts of violence erupted as screaming people were herded roughly through the double doors of the church – kicked and punched – a vicious rape here, a brutal beating there. Children clung fiercely to their mothers as entire families were brutally packed inside the town's most holy edifice. Once everyone was inside the small building, the German soldiers nailed the doors shut, trapping them inside.

Merciless, grim-faced men stood outside, rifles poised, machine guns at the ready, while other soldiers set the wooden church on fire, spitting vodka from their detestable mouths to feed the fast-rising, flickering flames.

This was their punishment for supporting our cause.

The sounds of their screams filled the air along with the crackling of the violent fire.

We were crouched in our hiding spot, tensed at the ready, but without the resources to combat a well-trained and well-armed German squad of about 50 soldiers.

As we watched helplessly in horror and everlasting grief, the entire village went up in flames. When the screams stopped, the church collapsed in the inferno and the Germans drove away.

There was nothing left to bury, nothing we could do. In shock, we left as well.

# VICTORY AT STALINGRAD

*February 2, 1943*

As February 1943 drew to a close, a contact lucky enough to own a working radio, told us the good news: the mighty German army had suffered a catastrophic defeat at Stalingrad. It was the turning point in the war, not just on the Eastern front, but the whole war.

Stalingrad is situated on the picturesque Volga, Russia's longest river. On February 2d the Russian army had finally penetrated the German lines at Stalingrad, located about one thousand miles east of our forest location, and all but destroyed them. The defeated German Sixth Army, unaccustomed to resounding defeat, had no choice but to surrender to their bitter enemies.

In one crushing sweep the Russians killed 110,000 Germans, captured 91,000 German prisoners of war and destroyed the Germans' supply lines. Though it was spring, the Russian weather was brutally cold and many German soldiers, cut off from supplies and reinforcements, froze to death.

The Russians assembled a massive artillery armada, two cannons per yard along the southeastern front. The Russians called their artillery "the mother of war."

That crushing defeat of the German Sixth Army at Stalingrad was the beginning of future German defeats along the Eastern front as the tide of the battle finally turned in our favor. The mighty German army had finally been beaten soundly, proving to us – and to the rest of the world – that they were not invincible; certainly not superior.

As partisan guerrillas and freedom fighters, and as young boys and young girls who had lived under German oppression for several years, now we celebrated. We rejoiced. We sang. We laughed. We joked. We cried. It felt good to have something to smile about. It cheered us to stand and grin and clasp each other's hands, simply enjoying the news about the Russians' major victory over the Germans. This gave us hope that someday, if we were somehow able to survive this struggle, if we could persevere in our fight for freedom, that we would eventually be liberated from German tyranny and become regular, normal people again. Civilians. Human beings. Jews.

In the meantime, the war was far from over. In many ways, for us, it was just beginning.

At this point there was no front on the ground in the west and Germany still controlled much of Europe. There was still much, much more to be done if we were to see real victory. We all knew that the Germans wouldn't go down without a fight.

Still, our exuberant celebration gave way to renewed resolve. For now, we knew that we had to destroy as many Germans and their collaborators as possible.

As winter ended and spring brought new life to the forest, we discovered a new enemy to fight: mosquitoes.

As the weather warmed and the snow started to melt, the humidity in the swampy regions of Polesie rose accordingly. Our secluded home, now muddy and damp, became a breeding ground for thousand of ravenous mosquitoes.

It was a minor problem at first. A nuisance. Annoying at best, hardly life-threatening. But as the spring advanced, their numbers increased and thick, huge clouds of mosquitoes soon plagued us from dawn to dusk. Inside the confines of our camp, with our continuous campfires, thankfully we could keep them at bay as the smoke seemed to deter them.

But when we went out on missions, the thick swarms of

mosquitoes became debilitating. It got so bad that we had to wear a patch of gauze over our mouths and noses to keep from breathing in the buzzing insects. If you opened your mouth to talk or breathe without the gauze to protect you, you soon enjoyed a dinner of fluttering mosquitoes. But we had a job to do and could not wear gauze all the time. Soon mosquito bites covered our bodies like angry, red freckles, causing us to itch and scratch. The local farmers gave us some lotion to smear on our faces, hands or any exposed part, which did bring big relief. Over time our bodies became immune. Nothing was going to keep us from our goals, not even swarms of pesky, flying mosquitoes.

However there was another difficulty brought by spring. In the winter the frozen swamps, lower water levels and thick snow enabled us to keep our horses, wagons and sleds inside our camp, which made it much easier to bring back supplies from our foraging expeditions.

But now as the snow melted and our swamp slowly liquefied, the thick oozing mud and brown, murky water made it impossible to use the horses and wagons. What we once used to throw casually in the back of a wagon, we now had to carry ourselves for as much as 5 miles from village to camp. Our packs grew bigger, our shoulders stronger, our backs more sore.

We became our own beasts of burden, which only added to the precariousness of each mission.

---

As our activities stepped up with the arrival of spring, we were more organized than ever. We established a central meeting place for the exchange of information between partisan groups. *"Blotko"* (little swamp), was so named because the location was a little island in the swamp, not far from the airfield and not far from Baranowicze, less than four miles from the city limits.

The partisans who gathered at the *blotko* also brought instructions on how to find places where other contacts were living. We used to send out men for the sole purpose of collecting information. There were times while on our way to a mission when we were able to stay with these "friends" for a few days, waiting for another contact to come with information that enabled us to complete the mission. The people who ran the *blotko* were from Baranowicze. They had been very rich before the war, but now they lived like the rest of us, in the swamps, making sacrifices.

We were all in it together.

Their brave hearts gave them the strength they needed to help the resistance movement in any way they could. The *blotko* was a godsend, a major development that increased our effectiveness and saved our lives in more ways than one. Our contacts would travel there and pick up or deliver information to the ghettos that still existed.

We were always hopeful that we would hear news of our families.

# THE DIRTY THIRTY

One day sometime toward the end of that blossoming March or at the beginning of April, we were greeted by a welcome sight: 3 broad, strong men showed up at the borders of our camp in the swamps. Unannounced. They were wearing Russian uniforms, modern guns slung over their shoulders, caps on straight, shoulders erect.

What a sight for sore eyes they were that fine spring day. Like a jolt of electricity, setting off a buzz of excitement around camp as word spread of the three visitors and the news that they might be bringing of the outside world. Little did we know how they would change our lives.

Escorted into partisan camp proper by our ever-watchful guards, the three men spoke forcefully, proudly, to our commandant Misha. They said they were part of a small group of elite Russian officers, members of a seven-man paratrooper company trained by the KGB. They had been dropped into the general area of our camp about a month before and had been scouting out various partisan camps since then. After all that time, of all the partisan groups operating in the vast territories of Belarus, they had picked our camp, our secluded, private campsite in the swamps because they liked the look and feel of the location.

Many considerations went into their choice. The density of the brush, the trees, the forest and, in particular, the "staggering amount" of clandestine operations we had engaged in, the amount of "noise" we had made, the success of our missions. The three Russian officers told us that Moscow had picked our forest as their drop site. It was their mission to build on the momentum that the forest partisans had gained, to reorganize partisan operations in our region and to handpick a group of 30 fighters to join their elite group to engage in even more sophisticated, daring and secretive operations.

The startling news brought murmurs and whispers to our camp and we respectfully listened while these men eyed us. Could it be true? Could Mother Russia have taken notice of *our* operations? Could our missions have been *that* successful? Could their confidence in the far-ranging partisan movement be so high that they would drop seven elite fighting machines into our midst to train us, mold us and shape us to be like them?

Our group fell into a large formation. One by one, the three Russian officers wound among us, moving from man to man, selecting as they went. A nod here, a point there; a whisper, a nudge. Every new recruit selected beamed.

We were a motley group to be sure. Standing there at attention in lines that weren't quite straight, rows that weren't quite formed and smiles that weren't quite trusting. Our bellies were empty, our clothes and faces dirty, but we stood tall and proud.

We were partisans. Dirty, smelly, tired, raggedy, fierce and hungry, but partisans just the same.

With guts! With courage!

I will never forget the immense feeling of pride that swept through me when I was chosen by one of the three Russian officers on that clear, spring day. I will never forget the thrill as I proudly joined twenty-nine other young men standing resolutely in rough formation. The chosen few. The select. We named ourselves "Brudna Trzydieska," the "Dirty Thirty."

There was barely time to grab our packs, say our goodbyes, as the Dirty Thirty were led through the dense forest to the paratrooper's mini-base camp. It was a very long trek, twenty forest miles, and took the rest of the day to reach.

When we arrived we could see that the paratroopers had chosen a beautiful pine forest, the "Mashuki Forest," as their initial base of operations. It was lush, green, thick and heady in the full throes of a springtime bloom that was as fragrant as it was picturesque. But despite its awe-inspiring beauty, those of us who had lived in the forest all winter knew that pine forests were not that safe, especially for the far-reaching and ambitious missions these brave men were planning.

Though the pine trees themselves grew tall and strong, reaching toward the sky with their fragrant needles and firm branches, no protective shrubs dotted the forest floor at their feet. There was simply nowhere to hide in such a pine forest.

Though the lush and lavish pine trees looked dense, stacked together as they were for miles and miles on end, you could still see clearly at least 100 feet or more from where you stood. And, if you could see that far, imagine how far the Germans who were looking for you could see!

In our old secluded swamp camp, so carefully chosen, so wisely selected, the protective birch trees were just as tall and strong as the fragrant pines. And the forest floor beneath their stretching branches was crowded with thick dense shrubs amidst the tall birch trunks. In our old camp, you couldn't see 10 feet from where you stood.

It was a small thing, this absence of shrubs, but it was distressing nonetheless. These were professional paratroopers, after all. The best of the best. The elite. The very best that the notorious Russian KGB had to offer. Decorated soldiers. Leaders. Didn't they know any better than to set up camp in a pine forest? Couldn't they see that they were practically sitting ducks?

My initial pride in being the youngest man chosen for this complex mission soon gave way to an alarming sense of fear and dread. As the hearty paratroopers guided us carefully into their camp, we, the Dirty Thirty, so honored in our hearts to have been chosen, now feared for our lives.

We were suddenly suspicious that these seven men, despite their stiff Russian uniforms, their well-oiled guns and their elaborate plans for the future of the partisan movement, were little more than crafty German spies sent to trick us, interrogate us, torture us and then kill us without mercy.

And so it was with a growing sense of dread that we gravely entered the pristine Russian camp and were formally introduced to the Russian general himself. His name was Orlowsky and he was a striking, yet tragic figure standing proud and tall in the midst of all those towering forest pines. The general had no arms! The captain had told us he had lost both of them on a daring mission to dynamite an important German train.

After meeting the general and falling under his spell, we were formally introduced to the rest of the paratroopers in the group: Colonel Niecolski, Captain Sania, Captain Ania (a doctor), Lieutenant Senia, Lieutenant Aliosha (the radio operator) and

Sergeant Peres (the general's valet).

They were all hearty men, well-trained, fit, regal in bearing, impressive in stature, decorated warriors all. Yet we feared them. Felt suspicious. Our guts warned us to be leery of them, to be fearful of German spies in our midst.

Tired from walking through the wilderness for almost eight hours to reach the camp, after awhile we decided to take a nap under a large tree, dozing while sitting up.

It was not a very restful sleep, however. Despite our weariness, despite all the excitement of our very eventful day, we all slept with one eye open.

When we awoke from our nap that first morning we were walking around with our heads hung, our shoulders hunched, our expressions grim, acting, walking and talking like zombies, much like we had in the ghetto.

It was as if the war had moved from the streets into our minds.

We decided that when we went to sleep that night, we would each take one hour shifts watching our Russian benefactors – or German executioners – as they slept. Around the clock. All night long. *Every* night. That way someone would be awake all the time and the German spies, if that's what they really were, wouldn't be able to surprise us.

After breakfast around the campfire, General Orlowsky noticed that we all looked gloomy and grim-faced. Like any good leader, he decided it was time for a pep talk; something to build morale, cheer our hearts, lift our heads.

He told us to assemble in the shape of a horseshoe so he could look each and every one of us in the eye as he spoke to us. As we did, we were prepared for the worst. When we were all assembled, in a firm, unwavering voice the Russian general said, "Why are you all so unhappy and gloomy? Look up to the sky and see its beauty."

He waited until we were all looking up into the vast springtime sky and then said, "It's a beautiful blue color and the sun is shining. The trees are standing tall and the ground is solid for you to walk upon."

Here he stomped his feet on the ground for emphasis before continuing: "All of these things are yours, they are free, you own them, so, please, don't be so gloomy. Be happy. Mother Russia is with you all the way!"

With that, the 30 of us looked hopefully from the blue sky and shining sun to the strong, tall trees, then down at the hard, firm ground that *was* ours to walk on. A few of us even stomped our feet imitating the general, *our* general.

It was *all* true. It was *ours*. We *deserved* it. We had *earned* it.

We had strived so much and fought so hard for so very long.

Better to be fighting. To live for another day and keep fighting. Always fighting. Wasn't that why we had risked everything to escape from Baranowicze? Yes, it *was* better. Better to trust these Russian officers with our lives and assist them in any way we could. Better that we should learn from them, soak up their knowledge, wisdom and experience, and then use it to fight the Germans even more fiercely.

Then, as if on cue, we gathered around the general and he let us listen to the radio. This was a true luxury. We did not have a radio. Not even Misha. All of our information had been provided by local farmers or villagers who owned radios.

After he turned the transmitter on, the radio crackled to life and we heard a message from the very heart of Moscow itself. It was an impassioned plea, delivered warmly and sincerely in Russian. It spoke of good tidings, of great things to come, wishing the partisans, wishing all of us, a good morning!

Surely this was no trick. Surely no German secret agents would go to such extremes to put on such an elaborate ruse. This was for real. It *had* to be. That was really Mother Russia on the radio, wishing us – wishing me, an eighteen year-old partisan straight off the streets of Baranowicze – a good morning! Urging us on, congratulating us, sending us wishes of goodwill and gratitude.

After the general had spoken with us and after that impromptu little ceremony that spring morning, we were issued the weapons we would use for the rest of the war. The Russian paratroopers gave each of us our own revolver, an automatic rifle, 3 extra magazines of 72 bullets each and 2 hand grenades.

It felt like a holiday.

That morning we officially became the Russian paratroopers' assistants or, as we liked to call ourselves, "mini-paratroopers." It was obvious that these seven Russian officers were wise beyond our years, seen things none of us could imagine and undergone training that might break the best of us.

It felt exciting to be in the midst of it all, to feel the heady rush of camaraderie and commitment now that we trusted them, now that we believed them. I could finally relax.

Almost immediately the men from our original group of 30 were assigned to small groups of 4, 5, or 6 men. We wasted no time and quickly began training for our missions. Our new assignments were to demolish bridges, derail freight trains and sabotage anything and everything that we could where the German army was concerned.

Three of us were assigned to guard the general himself – myself and two of my good buddies. We became his loyal bodyguards, charged with the task of protecting him at all times, both inside and outside camp.

The Dirty Thirty ranged in ages from eighteen to thirty-five. Some of the older men had served in the Polish army and were trained military men, already prepared to take on the more complicated missions.

The rest of us, who were little more than teenagers, made up for our lack of experience with courage, drive and determination. Perhaps it was in our blood, perhaps it was our brazen youth or perhaps it was just good, old-fashioned vengeance.

Either way, it worked.

# MEETING IN THE FOREST

One day around six in the morning I was on my way back from my first paratrooper mission with Captain Sania and Mishka, my old buddy from school. It had been successful; without incident, without casualties. The night before, we had destroyed a large factory that manufactured military uniforms for the German army; completely destroyed all the machinery and burned the wooden building to the ground. On top of this, with our silenced weapons, we also managed to kill two German soldiers guarding the premises.

It had taken two nights walking in swampy forest to reach the factory, one night to accomplish the mission and two nights walking back to our mini-camp. Walking in the woods, we talked as little as possible. Voices carried, so we always had to be careful.

All of a sudden we heard strange noises in the forest. Of course, during wartime, any noise in the forest is strange, but this time we knew the difference between normal forest noises, such as the croak of a bullfrog or the cracking of spring ice and ones that were foreign to our ears – a shoe stepping on a dry twig or the sliding of a rifle bolt. In a forest as dense and well-camouflaged as ours, many times our ears were better motion detectors than our eyes.

Guns at the ready, we called out, "Who goes there?"

The answer came from a voice in the forest, "It's us!"

This was unacceptable.

Sternly we demanded, "Give us the password!"

A partisan password was issued – and changed – every couple

of weeks to make it that much harder for the Germans to infiltrate our forest hideout.

Now, with fear and tensions running high, the unknown group in the forest responded with the correct password: "Forty-five."

There was a sigh of relief.

We invited them to come out of hiding and join us in the path between our side of the forest and theirs. In no time a small group of partisans came out to where we were standing: four men and one very beautiful woman. After exchanging greetings and the important news of the day, this group informed us that they, too, had just come from an operation and that their camp was about two miles away.

It was surprising to see a new group of faces so close to where our paratroopers had made camp. We had no idea this other group even existed, much less right down the road.

It seemed like a good reason to celebrate. We learned to relish the simple joys of momentary peace during wartime, and this was certainly one of those precious quiet moments. They invited us to their camp for dinner at 5 o'clock.

We accepted their invitation, got directions, returned to our mini-camp and reported our meeting to the general.

As dinnertime approached, we followed the directions to their camp. When Captain Sania, Mishka and I arrived, we were welcomed with open arms, just as we would have treated visitors to our camp. We were impressed with what we found.

There were over 100 members, both men and women. They seemed organized and efficient. Their camp was tidy, well-placed and secluded. Despite the lack of doors, walls, roofs, windows, teapots, pictures and tablecloths, good old-fashioned manners had refused to disappear from the Jewish way of life.

It was nice to be someone's guest, to meet interesting people, to see new faces, to exchange first names and funny stories and have the chance to ask about family, neighbors and friends. It didn't happen often. The camp buzzed with the lively sound of human conversation.

Fortunately for me, the most beautiful woman in the camp, the very girl that I had met hours earlier in the middle of the forest, came over and sat by my side throughout the evening. In-between polite laughter, we introduced ourselves.

"My name is Genia," she said shyly.

"I'm Munio," I said clumsily, explaining it was my nickname, the name the kids called me before the Germans invaded Poland.

Genia and I sat by the campfire and talked. She made me feel so at ease that it seemed as if I had known this beautiful woman all my life. We were so comfortable, joking and laughing; finding common ground in our home life and personal history, in our frame of reference and life experiences.

She and most of the other partisans in her camp had come from Baranowicze as well, and her escape had been just as daring as mine.

However Genia was fortunate enough to have her father and brother with her. In fact, her father was the leader of this partisan group, a strong, brave man whom I would come to love and respect almost as much as my own father.

His missions were not just for sabotage, but for rescue, too. He led missions into the ghetto to rescue people, take them out and bring them back to the forest. He was a true hero in every sense of the word.

For dinner they made fried potatoes. At that time under those conditions, a meal like that was a scarce luxury, a true delicacy, one that you made for important guests. A meal once taken for granted, a peasant's lunch, was now as precious and tasty as pheasant under glass.

The company was wonderful and the evening memorable. After dinner we said our goodbyes and went back to our own camp.

I felt a little sad leaving our new partisan friends, especially

Genia, who made me feel special.

But in a world of violence, uncertainty and sudden, senseless death, it was better not to get too close, it was better to remain distant, better to keep to yourself and avoid the pain and heartache that comes from meeting someone special only to lose them on a mission or in a deadly ambush.

The very next day our faithful contact warned us that the Germans had found out about partisan activities in our forest and were planning an all-out assault to clean out the forest once and for all.

With over 300 German soldiers armed to the teeth, headed our way, fully prepared to flush us out and kill every last one of us, there was no time to lose.

Their winter ambush had failed miserably; now they were hoping for better success in spring.

The general immediately ordered us to warn the newfound group of partisans, to join them and together with them move back to our original partisan camp as soon as possible. He sent me to tell them the plan of action, and I did so eagerly, walking those two miles faster than I'd ever walked in my life knowing that I'd be seeing Genia again.

I arrived at their camp at five in the morning. True partisans, they were ready in minutes and followed me to a pre-arranged meeting point halfway between our mini-camp and theirs.

There, in the middle of the forest where we had both operated without knowing the other existed, we met up with my paratrooper unit, and together we all tramped through the deep, dark woods back to our original camp, where Misha's partisans were.

The general's move was a good one. A wise choice. We knew the area from living there earlier in the winter and would lose no time finding our way around. It was also far enough away from our current camp to be safe and still had all the bunks we had originally built to keep dry and warm.

It was a long walk to our old camp, over twenty miles, and Genia and I walked side by side the entire way.

I had been on many missions and walked many a mile during my time as a partisan. Most such journeys were extremely quiet and dull, punctuated rarely by the occasional bad joke or latest rumor of war. But this march was entirely different.

Genia and I talked as mile after mile passed blissfully beneath our feet. We talked about everything and we talked about absolutely nothing. It was nonstop conversation the whole way.

Too soon we reached our camp. My former commandant, Captain Misha, and our old partisan group welcomed us warmly and we introduced them to the general and the rest of the paratroopers.

We had to clean out the bunks, which had grown musty. The work went smoothly, with many hands contributing to the greater good, and soon we were settled into our new, old camp once again. The group easily merged into one.

It was our turn to play host and we greeted our guests with the best kind of news. Safely secluded but ever alert, we soon heard from our loyal contact that the German ambush had been unsuccessful and that all 300 of them had gone away empty-handed and extremely frustrated.

We celebrated by gathering around the campfire each night, sharing old stories with our new friends and singing songs, aware that our fortuitous meeting in the forest had saved over a 100 Jewish lives.

A chance meeting that brought me the satisfaction of doing good work and finding a girlfriend as well.

I had not yet recovered from the disillusionment of my failed relationship with Sima, who had made me look like a fool to my close friends, and I felt suspicious of girls. And I had met a nice girl, actually a young woman a little bit older. I was eighteen, she was twenty-one, but I was chicken and afraid to start anything because I had been burned before.

With Genia, though, it was different and we began seeing each other; that is, unofficially. We practiced a mix of traditional, older values combined with newer ideas based on the hazardous nature of partisan life. Genia was an older woman, which, up to this point, would have been taboo for a teenager like me. Yet as our friendship grew stronger, a feeling decidedly stronger than friendship blossomed between us.

Her father Judel helped us in our awkward courtship, even though I don't believe he ever realized it.

Judel was a World War II hero and an inspiration to us all. Each night we would gather around the campfire and he would regale us with tales of adventure. Unlike partisans like ourselves and the paratroopers who engaged exclusively in missions directly affecting the Germans, Judel had devoted his life as a partisan warrior rescuing Jews from the ghetto and small labor camps. Single-handedly he brought about 12 Jewish people out of the ghetto on each mission, and had saved well over 100 men, women and children from certain death.

I was inspired by his nightly stories of heroism and derring-do and aimed to follow in his enormous footsteps if that was possible. He made me hope that one day I, too, could go on a mission to help rescue Jews – my father, my mother, my little brother and my friends.

When Judel wasn't telling war stories, he was also a great *kibitzer* as was his son Max. Each night the comedy team of Judel and Max told jokes and made us forget about our dreary situation. The entire camp looked forward to the evening's fireside "chats."

I did, too. But I had a different reason for anticipating the evening.

Genia was my constant fireside companion whenever I was in camp between missions. She had a beautiful singing voice and was often accompanied by the accordion. She would start singing, someone else would join in and we would be treated to a beautiful duet.

After the yarn spinning, joke telling and the singing there were quiet times for Genia and myself. More than any of it, more than all of it, I longed for these times at the campfire with Genia. The memories of our evenings together and the anticipation of our next meeting kept me going.

Because there was always another mission to go on.

And another. And then another.

# AIR DROPS

Two new paratroopers joined our camp toward the end of spring. One was a major and the other a "half-doctor" by the name of Max. In Russia, Poland and other countries there were many such half-doctors. We called them "felchers." A felcher is a professional with two years of medical school. Not yet a "real" doctor, but more than a registered nurse, felchers can perform certain medical duties and write certain prescriptions. In camp they took care of our minor wounds and illnesses.

With these two new Russian officers we now had a total of nine paratroopers, the Dirty Thirty mini-paratroopers and about 250 assorted partisans, resisters and freedom fighters in our main camp in the swamps of Polesie.

We had managed to amass a fierce, passionate and loyal group of nearly 300 people, almost all of them Jewish partisans. It was large enough to become an actual brigade. Officially, it was known as the "paratroopers group," or "The Orlowsky Brigade," after our illustrious Russian general.

The brigade was divided in three groups: the Russian

officers and paratroopers, we Dirty Thirty assistant paratroopers and Captain Misha and the partisans

The food missions were assigned to Misha's group, which also helped on paratrooper assignments and parachute drops.

The mini-paratroopers were directly involved with the Russian paratroopers' actions: spying, destroying railroad tracks, bridges, military warehouses and communication systems; ambushing trucks, "disposing of" SS and Gestapo officers and military personnel and "getting rid of" spies and collaborators.

We began having radio contact with Moscow a few times a day. The central region in our forest was very convenient to their base of operations, which was an important reason for selecting us to join their elite group of fighting paratroopers.

---

At the end of April the Russians began flying in a supply plane every four weeks. These were dangerous missions for the Russians. They had to be accomplished with the utmost secrecy and always in the dead of night. Still, there was no easy way to hide a Russian war plane careening in and out of the forest in the middle of the night.

Each air drop exposed us to great danger.

To keep the German army off balance and confuse them, we never used the same location or time for a drop more than once. Every time a supply plane prepared for another drop, we steered it to a different place at a different time. Because we knew the forest best, the paratroopers and mini-paratroopers generally chose the place.

These supply planes were crucial to the new era of partisan actions and provided us with such necessities as automatic rifles, revolvers, ammunition and explosives; salt, sugar and tobacco and medicine, too. Once the Russian paratroopers learned of our problem with lice and typhus, the drop also included a healthy supply of special powder that killed the lice instantly. Once in a while they would even include true luxuries like matches, soap and candy. The Russian planes some times made a drop in another location for another partisan brigade.

Crucial supplies were dropped into the forest attached to white parachutes to cushion their descent. Some times the wind was a big problem, sending the drops way off course. In such cases we were always afraid that German troops might spot them first and be lying in wait to pepper us with machine-gun fire.

The parachute drops required strict planning, both on the ground and in the air. The day before, our paratrooper leaders would give the pilots strict instructions about the secret location. The next day, 24 mini-paratroopers and a few paratroopers would prepare the drop zone, and then anxiously await the arrival of the Russian supply plane.

We usually selected a site in an open field between two forests about three hundred feet apart. This increased the chances of the parachutes landing on open ground instead of getting hung up in any of the towering trees that surrounded the zone. Every moment we spent collecting supplies exposed us to the threat of German intervention, so we planned for the least amount of exposure and the most amount of safety.

The Dirty Thirty, a few paratroopers and some of Misha's partisans – 48 men in all – were involved in these deadly missions every four weeks. Additionally, 24 well-armed partisans from Misha's group were stationed in the adjoining forest and covered our backs: they were ready to protect us in the event the Germans spotted us and began an attack; they were to cover us – with their eyes, their ears and their guns.

As part of the preparation for these daring night drops, each of us carried a bottle of kerosene with a knot of rope dangling inside the bottle to light when it was almost time for the drop.

This was a visual signal that the pilots could see from the air.

At night when the planes came, the bottles worked like little lanterns. We made an airfield runway by forming 2 lines, 12 men in each line standing side by side 50 feet apart. All of us risking our lives to be there, those in the air and those on the ground. Getting in and getting out was the motto of the day for pilots and partisans alike. We worked quickly, with deadly precision under tight deadlines, urging each other on, pressing, faster, faster. The 48 of us – partisans, paratroopers and minis – were well-trained and expertly rehearsed in this type of mission. We also had a group of "understudies" in camp, just in case we needed them.

This speed, this determination to leave the area immediately after a drop, drastically reduced the risk of our being detected.

We had the greatest respect for these daring Russian pilots.

At a given time the mission captain would signal us to light the lanterns. Like magic, the makeshift "runway" would spring to life and the roaring cargo plane above would drop its silken parachutes.

Seeing 24 partisans light their lanterns all at once was quite an experience, both breathtaking and unforgettable.

Immediately after we saw the bags drop, we'd blow the lanterns out. Then we would wait a little while longer to make sure that we had no interference, that there were no Germans lurking to ambush us as we collected the supplies.

While the pilot's job was over, it was still a very stressful time for those of us on the ground.

When everything was finally quiet in the dark forest and we felt confident that we were reasonably safe, we would pick up the bags and disappear into the surrounding trees and shrubs as quickly as we could.

Our burden was heavy to be sure, but the adrenaline from being exposed to deadly German eyes filled our muscles with unexpected strength and energy.

The walk back to camp was often long, between three and four hours. This was on purpose. Should the Germans discover and ambush us, they would still be an extremely long distance from our base camp and unable to find it.

While the trip might have been long and dangerous – it was well worth the risk to protect the rest of the partisans – those supplies kept us going, kept us alive; fighting, destroying, diverting and killing.

The 24 of us had 12 parachutes between us. Two men would carry one bag and a chute for about a half hour or so and then we would switch and let the two men who had been resting carry it for awhile so that we in turn could rest.

To share the weight of the load, we would have the chute hanging off our shoulders on a long branch, the bag dangling between us, like a sling between our shoulders. This was easier than hoisting the heavy bags on our shoulders for the entire journey.

These operations were extremely dangerous and we were always on the lookout for unwelcome surprises. The weapons increased our effectiveness as guerrilla fighters, giving us two, three and sometimes four times the firepower we had had before, not to mention the medicine and the other supplies that made living in the forest more bearable, like the lice powder.

These operations were not only a crucial part of our survival but also of the survival of all the others who depended upon us. Some of those supplies were distributed to other partisan groups in the area as well.

During one operation, the big German guns actually shot down one of the Russian planes as it prepared to make its drop. In shock and panic, we stood frozen on the ground, watched it explode into pieces and fall from the air, losing sight of the burning wreckage as it disappeared behind the distant tree line. Once it did, we split up and disappeared into the trees ourselves, ignoring the massive explosion at our backs and running for our lives. Fortunately the German guns missed all the partisans on the ground.

But, without that drop, our supplies ran low, making us more aware than ever just how important these nighttime drops were. They were crucial to our survival.

There was grief in our hearts for the Russian pilots who had risked and ultimately lost their lives aiding our war effort.

And there was fear in our hearts for our own lives.

But to keep disrupting the German army, to keep up the fight, to keep "making noise," as we called it, the missions had to go on.

The drops had to continue.

# THE WARSAW GHETTO UPRISING

*Passover 1943*

In keeping with their traditional tactic of turning Jewish holidays into days of mourning, the Nazis scheduled the final deportation of the remaining 60,000 Jews on Passover.

But when the Germans arrived at the ghetto at 3 a.m. they were unexpectedly met with armed resistance and had to retreat.

The ghetto survivors, knowing there was no hope of victory and little hope of survival, had decided to take a stand. With no help from the Polish underground, this Jewish Resistance lasted until May 16th – for 27 days – longer than it had taken the well-armed Germans to conquer all of Poland.

The news trickled in from our various contacts and from the radio supplied by our Russian partners. A few thousand Jews managed to escape and joined us in the forest. We shared their sorrow, felt their pain. They were us and we were them.

Before the war began, before the ghetto was established, before the German soldiers began their unrelenting campaign of death, the Jews had lived in Warsaw.

It was beyond belief, beyond human comprehension to fathom that the Nazi executioners had killed over 500,000 human beings. But we who had lived through the extermination of the Baranowicze ghetto, not once but twice, could certainly believe it. And those Jews who had lived through other massacres in other ghettos, who lost their family members, could certainly believe it, too. It was the same hell on earth we had all experienced, but on a much larger scale.

It was simple mathematics to the Germans: 5,000 in this ghetto, 15,000 in that ghetto and another 500,000 over in Warsaw.

It was death, super sized.

---

Our missions fighting in the forest continued with increasing momentum. We were not always successful, we did not always triumph and not all of us who left always returned.

On one mission in a small town, German soldiers ambushed 3 of us, a paratrooper captain and two of us "minis." We had destroyed the German post office, with the telephone and telegraph stations inside. In those days, the telephone, telegraph and post office were all located in the same building. To make a call or send a telegram, soldiers had to go to the post office. By cutting the cables to this one building, communication to Germany, or anyplace else, was effectively stopped. Naturally this was a very important and dangerous type of partisan sabotage.

Fortunately there was only one casualty during this particular mission.

Unfortunately that casualty was me!

Once we saw what was happening, once we heard the German soldiers shouting at our backs, cursing us and threatening our lives, once the bullets started flying overhead and underfoot, we began running out of the town, scattering in our usual pattern, one running this way, one running that way, the third running away from the other two.

The Germans continued shooting, their machine-gun fire following us as we scattered. I had lived by the motto "He who runs the fastest, lives the longest." But this time I guess I was running fast enough to get away, but not fast enough to avoid getting shot. With a searing hot flash of pain, one of the Germans' bullets hit my arm.

I couldn't stop to examine and dress my wound, apply bandages or seek medical assistance. I couldn't stop and catch my breath, tear off a part of my shirt and wrap it around the wound like a tourniquet to stem the bleeding. I had to keep running.

With bullets slamming into tree trunks to my right and into the soft dirt beneath me, I ran on, feeling the warm blood trickle down my cold, clammy arm.

I didn't know how bad the wound was or if it was life-threatening. I only knew that it hurt. And that I was scared. Scared I might lose my arm.

When I finally reached camp and received medical attention, I found out that the wound wasn't too bad. Luckily the bullet had only penetrated the fleshy part of my soft muscle. With rest and proper attention, my arm healed completely in a month.

When I thought about it later, I realized how fortunate I was that I hadn't been killed that day. Although I was not a religious boy, I do believe a higher power must have been watching over me, as it had throughout the war.

How many times had my life been spared? How many close calls had I had? How many bullets had whizzed past my head? Finding life in "this" line while others found death in "that" line? Hiding in an outhouse at just the right time, watching others find death in another roundup, another slaughter?

How many lives did I have left?

---

After the deadly German ambush, we uprooted ourselves and moved our entire camp to another location even deeper in the forest. To a bigger island in the swamps, better hidden and harder to navigate.

This time the camp was surrounded by even more trees, more foliage and even more Jewish sympathizers in the form of watchful farmers and villagers nearby.

But now we were a group of about 300 loyal resistance fighters, 260 partisans and 39 paratroopers. The new camp was built much like the old one. There were ten bunks for sleeping, one bunk consisting of a large space for the kitchen, two bunks for men's and women's bathrooms, a special bunk for the paratroopers and the radio transmitter, a special bunk for the mini-paratroopers and two bunks for a hospital, since we now had two doctors in our group: a man who had escaped from the ghetto, and the woman paratrooper who was a captain.

It felt good to have proper medical attention at last. Not just for minor things like mosquito bites and poison ivy, but for bloody bullet wounds.

But, even as fortunate as we were, to have a well-trained medical staff, some times a doctor with limited resources wasn't able to repair damage that was too serious, too far gone.

One day 10 of us were assigned to cut trees in the forest. We had to prepare wood for the campfires, for the bunk drums and for use in the kitchen for cooking.

While foraging for wood, I looked over and saw two men cutting down a tree.

When the tree was ready to fall, when we heard the creaking of its trunk straining against the stump in the ground, I noticed one of the men, Kivelewicz, standing in its path. I started screaming for him to move out of the way, but he did not hear me. Instead, he froze.

The tree hit him directly on the head.

The doctors came and got him. He died a few days later. This was a terrible loss to us all. He had survived three slaughters in the ghetto, withstood numerous assaults by the Nazis, been tortured, beaten, brutalized and betrayed. And now he had been killed by something as stupid and careless as a falling tree. Where the brutal and senseless forces of war had not been able to take his life, Mother Nature and the whims of chance and place, had.

We cut up the tree that had killed him and used it for firewood.

# HATRED AND REVENGE

My mantra, my driving thought for much of 1942, 1943 and 1944 was "Hatred is a terrible thing. But who taught us how to hate?"

These are the words I spoke to myself over and over again, each and every morning as a partisan. They weren't very nice or neat. They weren't very comforting. But I meant every single one of them.

My fellow Jews and I had so much hatred built up in our hearts, so much animosity, so much pain, that at times it was almost unbearable. *Almost.*

But why *wouldn't* we hate? How *couldn't* we? And more importantly, why *shouldn't* we? Those brutal German bastards had savagely killed our families: our fathers, our mothers, our brothers and our sisters; our loved ones, our neighbors and our friends.

They had annihilated the Jews in our once-beautiful town.

Yet as much as those German murderers had done to us, as much as they had stolen from us, as much as they had put us through, we managed to overcome.

Hatred is a terrible thing.

It gnawed at our bellies like a growing cancer. It rolled around in our heads like marbles. It whispered in our ears as we marched through the forest on missions as dangerous as they were necessary. Night and day, we thought of revenge and destruction and mayhem and death.

It consumed us, keeping us awake when we were exhausted and should have been sleeping. We had been a very peaceful, private people before the war. Now we were haters, slayers and killers.

Just like them.

But we had a good reason: REVENGE!

Not only had they brutalized us, tortured us and killed us, but the German army had also turned the Jews into a new breed of soldiers who fought, who blew things up, who killed, who did things never before imagined and who hated – who hated all the Jew haters!

Our goal was still to destroy as many German murderers and their treasonous accomplices as possible before they killed *us*.

At this time the German army was still a strong force, but

Hitler's personal army was getting weaker. We knew that they were losing the war. We knew that Allied Forces were finally making advances in territories formerly occupied by Germany.

The question now was *when*?

When would they lose the war?

When would their reign of terror, death and destruction finally end?

But the biggest, scariest, most important question of all was, Would we still be alive when it was all over?

Unfortunately the bitter and severe hatred we all felt for the German army and their vicious accomplices did not detract from our crippling fear.

It often came rushing back to us that we were still only children, teenagers really, toting guns and firing them, weighted down with grenades and targets to assassinate.

Naturally we were still scared to death every time we had to go on one of these dangerous missions. After receiving our packet of detailed instructions, maps and targets, our commandant would always give us a little "pep talk."

While other boys our age in other parts of the world got pep talks before football, basketball or soccer games, we got pep talks before heading off to blow-up bridges, cut down phone lines or perhaps assassinate someone.

It was a strange and brutal existence.

Once we left the camp on a mission, the fear would disappear and that cold, boiling hatred would take over.

Hatred toward Hitler.

Hatred toward the Germans.

Hatred toward German sympathizers.

Hatred toward the gentiles who had helped the Germans seek us out.

Hatred toward those forces that wished to murder and eradicate us.

It's a terrible thing to fear death. Sudden, brutal, violent and bloody death. Right around the corner just past that tree in that field, caught in the path of a whizzing bullet you didn't see or impaled by a soldier's knife so sharp it cut to the bone before you realized it.

I often wondered, Is this mission the one? The one where they get me? The one where I die? How will it happen? An ambush? A surprise? Will it be during the mission? An explosion? Will it happen on the way back? Will they stab me? Shoot me? Or drop a mortar round in the middle of our entire group of five, six, seven or more partisans? Will it feel any better dying with my comrades than dying alone in a pool of my own blood? Will I be captured? Tortured? Buried alive? Starved to death? Hanged?

Dying would not matter so much as long as we could take a few of those German killers with us. It sounds macho to say it now, almost unbelievable, but at the time, it was our grim reality.

In some ways it might have been a relief, for what did we have left? No home to go back to. No street address. No city. No country.

We had the clothes and rifles on our backs, the pistols in our holsters, a little food in our bellies and a mission. Always another mission.

That was it.

That was all.

That was what passed for life in times of war.

Was it so terribly strange to have a death wish when your life was little more than a living death?

At times we felt that we had already been killed, so much death had occurred, so many murders, so many tortures, so many rapes and so many atrocities.

"If I live, I'll see you tomorrow. If not, I'll see you the next day." *That* attitude helped each of us to be brave.

# HOPE FOR RESCUE

To my surprise, one day through one of our contacts in Baranowicze, I received a letter from my mother Sara. It was a godsend; a brave act of smuggling by the man who delivered it.

I read and re-read it, over and over again. My mother and my little brother Jackob were still alive. In words both tragic and hopeful, my mother said that they had been the last few to survive the third and final slaughter in Baranowicze and, considering everything that had happened, were in pretty good shape.

They were still working at that nearby brick factory. They were able to work side by side, slept in the same bunk and clinged to each other in the cold night. No small comfort to be sure, but one that I knew would be greatly appreciated by both my mother and my little brother, barely ten years old.

My mother said that she had been longing to see me, and in words that somehow managed to break my heart, that she could "hardly wait for the moment to come" when she would see me.

She also said, "It's in your power to take us from here sooner…"

She signed it, "Your loving mother who wants to see you soon."

Several long and doleful days passed after I received this letter, which brought equal measures of comfort and distress. Commandant Misha noticed the sudden change in me. Usually extroverted and gregarious among the troops, I could barely exchange greetings with my fellow partisans.

One blue and lonesome day as I sat staring at my battered shoes and could barely lift my head, Misha stopped and asked me what was wrong. It's a tribute to Misha's wisdom and sensitivity that with all that was going on in our lives, he could still tune into me.

I told him about my mother and my little brother, about the letter that, at once, offered so much hope and so much dread.

Misha, a very good man and a kind human being, said he would see what information he could gather. But he did much more.

He was able to get in touch with a partisan contact near Baranowicze, and told him to find a way to get my family out of the brick factory.

A few days later the contact replied: he could probably arrange for their escape, but would need 25,000 rubles (about $100) to pay the man who could accomplish this task.

Without hesitation Misha offered to give me the money, with no strings attached. He told me to pick three other men with relatives in the labor camp in Baranowicze who would be willing to take this assignment and go meet the contact.

Excited to finally be going on a mission to save my family, I quickly selected three partisans: my friend, Itche, who had an uncle alive in a labor camp, and two other friends. The commandant then gave me instructions, who to contact and what to say and wished us a safe return.

And just like that, a mission I had dreamed about since I had escaped – rescuing my own – was happening.

Heading toward Baranowicze, the 4 of us came to a crossroads. Our instructions were to take the road to the right. However as commander of the group, I decided to use the road to the left instead, just to get some experience on the other side of the airfield that we were skirting in case we ever needed to use it.

It took us a night's travel to reach our destination. When we arrived at the meeting place the next day, the *blotko* a few miles from Baranowicze, our contact, "Hatio," informed us that four other partisans had been killed the day before, ambushed by the Germans. Where? we asked. He said: At the crossroads, on the road to the right.

Hatio was the man who would bring my mother and brother out of the factory. He eagerly took our money and just as eagerly assured us that it wouldn't be long before he freed my mother and my little brother. For now, however, we all had to stay at the *blotko* and wait.

A few days passed. Finally we received news that a woman, a child and my friend's uncle had escaped and were on their way to meet us.

I was excited and nervous.

Though I felt confident that the stranger we had met at the *blotko* would be true to his word, to learn that he had actually been successful brought a flutter to my heart – and tears of gratitude to my eyes.

From what I had been told by our contacts, my mother and my little brother knew where I was and had been planning to escape and join me.

Secretly, and perhaps a little foolishly under the present circumstances, I was already making plans for their triumphant arrival; imagining the three of us together again. Cast into the violent sea of war, linked by blood, still praying for the best, but fearing the worst.

In my mind I had already started planning for my father's escape as well. Three of us would not be complete. Nothing short of a true reunion would do. It must be the four of us, the entire Lato family back together again.

So it was that I almost fainted when a strange woman and child – not my mother and not my little brother – walked into the *blotko* several days later.

How eager I had been to see them again, to touch them, to hear them, to hold them in my arms and to keep them safe. This was not to be. How foolish I had been. How naïve.

All of my plans had failed.

I was destroyed; hysterical.

I felt as though I had just lost my mother and my little brother all over again for a second time. My family, my blood, my life! I felt as if they had slipped from my reach. The days, weeks and months of mental toughness that I had built up, the distance that I had put between myself and my deepest, darkest feelings, all crumbled in the blink of an eye. My heart was broken; aching terribly.

When I finally managed to calm down a little, a very little, the contact who had brought the strange woman and child told me what had happened: someone had double-crossed my family, betrayed them at the last minute.

Someone in the factory had found out who the man was who was going to bring my mother and brother out. That person offered him more money to trade my mother and brother for two other people. It was a common practice on the brutal black market of human commerce.

And, as I had expected, feared and dreaded, the Germans would seek retribution when they found out that two Jews had escaped and that two more – my mother and my little brother – had planned to escape.

Knowing full well what would hurt them the worst, what would cause them to suffer the most; my mother was then separated from my little brother and put in a different work group.

They were even separated at night, forced to say goodbye after a grueling day of labor, placed in different bunks and denied each others comfort. Oh how that must have killed her! My darling little brother ripped from my mother's arms. Worst of all, their hopes for another chance at escape had been irrevocably dashed.

They were *not* coming.

Not my mother.

Not my little brother.

Not this time.

Maybe not ever.

## TRANSLATION

*My dear son, I received your letter, my dear son. You have no idea, my love, how comforting it is to know that you are ok and feeling fine. I can hardly wait for the happy moment to come when I see you. I do not know how to make it happen but I will try my best. I am trying to meet with comerade H. Yackob and I are working very hard but the situation is not good. It's in your power to take us from here sooner. Dear Muka is probably there with Abram and Ieronis.*

*Love you my dear and send you a kiss. Also say hi to everybody I know. Say hi to Mukasiey from Franka, she is waiting to hear from him. See you soon, your loving mother who wants to see you soon.– Mother*

The letter from my mother, Sara telling me she wants to see me and that she wants me to take her and my little brother Jackob out from the ghetto as soon as I can. Partisan Time, Belarus 1943. Letter is written in Russian.

# MISSION 1: TOLL OF WAR

The failed rescue weighed on me and I carried a heavy heart that ached for my dear mother and my little brother. I prayed silently for them and for my father. For myself, too.

Our activities stepped up. This helped. I felt more determined than ever. I knew that the only way to help our cause, any cause, was to disrupt the Germans as quickly as possible at every turn.

One night 3 of us were assigned to dispose of a dangerous German collaborator, a harmful informer and treacherous spy.

We came to a village, found the house, knocked and asked the man who answered the door his name. When he said the right name, we knew he was *that* collaborator.

Without another word, the captain raised the silenced pistol that he was holding at his side and put a bullet in the collaborator's head. He then put his pistol back in his holster and we ran. We had no trouble, no casualties. Because of this collaborator, many decent farmers had been killed by the Germans. So the captain killed him. He was the enemy. It was as simple as that.

After that no one in that village was killed by the Germans.

On another occasion, I was part of a group of 32 partisans and a few paratroopers, selected to go on a mission to raid a large German supply warehouse. Our contact gave us clear instructions. We found the warehouse a few days later, broke in quietly at night, dispatched post-haste the lone policeman, loaded our wagons with the goods we needed and left in a hurry.

As always the mission was the easier part – the dangerous part was getting home alive.

After traveling for a few hours on our way back, we stopped in the forest to rest. Since it was secluded and a good place to set up a camp, we decided to stay until the next night. Everybody went to sleep. I stayed up and sat by the campfire.

There was no particular reason why I stayed up except for a funny feeling I had in the pit of my stomach. Like a premonition telling me *not* to go to sleep. Something about that night, that location, that mission made me feel different, a bit strange. So, despite my weariness, I never dozed off. I was cautious and alert.

As sunrise approached I started to boil potatoes for breakfast. It was common partisan fare and by now I had gotten quite good at making this dull staple taste good. I woke up my cousin Israel, who happened to be on this mission, and asked him if he wanted to eat. Surprisingly, he declined, saying he wanted to sleep a little longer.

After a few minutes I looked up and saw German soldiers heading our way. It wasn't long before they saw me as well! Immediately they all started screaming, shouting for us to surrender and when we didn't, the Germans began shooting. Bullets were flying everywhere, the forest erupting with gunfire from every direction.

I left everything right where it was – the pans, the potatoes – and ran as fast as I could. We all did; partisans on the left and on the right, springing to life and disappearing in the forest.

As I was running away from the Germans, a spray bullet knocked my cap off my head, sending it flying through the air. But I was not hit or hurt.

I quickly caught up to the four other men from our mission and we ran together. We stumbled into a small partisan camp and the five of us stayed there for the rest of the day and night dressing our mental wounds. We were afraid that we were the only survivors. At sunrise, when the forest was clear of Germans, a few partisans from the other camp joined us and we retraced our steps, looking for survivors.

We found 8 more of our men and 2 paratroopers. They were in shock, just wandering around, dazed and confused, but thankfully unharmed from the hail of gunfire. We surmised that the Germans had found those who had been wounded and simply finished them off.

We then spread out and began the grim task of looking for bodies. It was an odious task, searching the forest floor for trails of blood, guts and gore. Looking for the faces of our friends, searching for their tattoos, their boots, their caps, their packs, their jackets and their guns.

We would find 17 dead bodies that day, one of them my young and handsome cousin Israel. I felt as if someone had kicked me in the stomach when I recognized him. He had taken bullets in the head and chest. Here was a boy who had survived after escaping from the Baranowicze ghetto with his brother Abraham. Here was a boy who had risked it all, who had played dead on the cold ground as German soldiers stripped him of his clothes and a policeman fired a bullet straight at his head and missed. And for what . . .

We hoisted Israel's lifeless body and carried him tenderly to dry ground for a proper burial. But the members of that small partisan group suggested that we go right back to our own camp. They were tactful in their choice of words, ever respectful of our loss of our dear friends and even offered to bury our fallen comrades in a safe dry spot for us.

In the midst of our sorrow and loss, they had realized that it would have been too difficult for us. We were grateful for their offer. We felt that remaining behind to bury the bodies of our fallen friends was the least we could do. Two paratroopers, a few of the men and I stayed behind until all our casualties were buried.

In addition to our 17 comrades, we had lost 5 of our horses and wagons that were full of valuable supplies.

Heartbroken, devastated, depressed and exhausted, we thanked the other partisans for all of their help and went back to our camp. We never saw them again.

Like a mirage, they appeared out of nowhere then disappeared.

Once again I had survived a deadly ambush and lived to see another day while so many of my comrades had fallen; some who had been standing right next to me.

---

Back at camp I noticed that my walking boots were literally falling apart. Walking and running through swamps and forests had ruined them. Although it may sound like a trivial matter considering all the death and destruction we encountered on a daily basis, a partisan's boots were no laughing matter. My boots carried me on every mission, through fields and forests, cities and towns. Without my boots, I could not have escaped.

Fortunately a farmer from a nearby village who had become a good friend gave me a pair of his old boots. While the tops were in pretty good shape, I knew the bottoms wouldn't last much longer. Making the most of what I had, I took the two pairs of boots apart and matched the tops with a new bottom made of rich, soft leather.

I remembered making the ice skates in trade school, and that professor who thought it was a bad idea. What I was doing now wasn't going to win me any contests, but it was going to keep my feet warm and comfortable, help keep me alive. Maybe the lesson was being practical.

I cut the piece of soft leather to fit the old boot tops and sewed them by hand. Then I gave the top part of the boots and some hard leather to a shoemaker in a nearby village and asked him to make a new bottom for me.

Using this rough combination of old and new, the shoemaker then made an entirely "new" pair of boots for me. As a result of the soft leather and the shoemaker's careful craftsmanship, I almost never had any blisters on my feet – a blessing to a walking partisan. The new boots were also waterproof, perfect for the always wet and damp conditions of our swampy camp, and would serve me extremely well.

I could not have chosen a better time to repair my boots as the guerrilla warfare suddenly intensified.

Every mission presented a new challenge and every target had its own set of predetermined rules.

Some missions were all prelude. The Germans had a thriving lumberyard in a small community near Baranowicze. Since I worked there for a few weeks when I lived in the ghetto, I was given the assignment of destroying it. It was a 4-man team, three minis and a paratrooper who was expert in explosives.

Seeing this lumberyard again brought up a lot of feelings, but there was no time for the past. Staying alive meant staying in the present, in the moment.

We did night reconnaissance and investigated the conditions of the plant. Nothing could be left to chance. We never assumed anything. It took six days to plan the operation and less than fifteen minutes to blow this lumberyard up in a roaring fire.

Having worked there under the Germans, I took special pleasure demolishing it. I knew that my father would have felt great pride in this achievement.

Another day three of us were dispatched to a nearby town where we destroyed a German bakery, stopping production – and delivery – of fresh baked goods to German soldiers. Since the bakery was made of logs, it burned quickly. We also made sure that the ovens were destroyed. Our goal was always maximum damage.

We continued to hit the Germans' supply lines. A warehouse whose workers were sympathetic to the German cause, where they made uniforms and provided supplies to the Germans, was also firebombed.

As the Germans began tasting bitter defeats more regularly, changes were occurring in the partisan camps as well. The biggest one that affected me personally was General Orlowsky being recalled back to Moscow.

In the days just after the general was gone, I missed him tremendously. He and I had formed a strong bond. He used to call me "gimnasist," not Samuel. In Russia, a "gimnasist" is a high school graduate. Like Captain Misha, he had been my leader, my mentor and my friend.

Mishka and I were assigned to Colonel Niecolski.

There were changes in the missions, too. Because of our successes, we had to go farther and farther on our excursions and the missions themselves became more erratic, more scattered.

We could tell that the end was coming.

# THE LITTLE GREEN FOREST

When they first occupied our little town of Baranowicze, the Germans used to force the Jews to dig ditches in the forest by the little green railroad bridge. Eventually we found out that the purpose of these ditches was for mass graves for the Jews who, at a later date, would be brought there and murdered – their final act, falling into their own graves.

These graves were not far from the forest which gave us cover as we went on missions to try to save some of the unlucky Jews fated to die there.

We called this pine forest outside of Baranowicze "the grind weldl," or "the little green forest." It's where the Germans, along with their accomplices, would kill and bury 100,000 Jews during the course of the war.

Some local farmers, who were gentiles, took advantage by stealing from the Jews on the way to their deaths, helping the

Germans in any way they could.

Even out of this death and destruction, though, while most perished, some survived.

There were many "little green forests" in Poland.

One night, while sitting around the fire, one such survivor, Cherna Curkoff, told us of the slaughter in her hometown of Kletzk in late October 1942. With tears in her eyes and sometimes crying, she recounted the horror.

The German Wermacht had surrounded the ghetto and assembled all the Jews at the market square in the middle of town. There, trucks were waiting to be loaded, to take them to the already-prepared mass graves in the forest outside of Kletzk.

Once the German trucks and their human cargo arrived at the mass gravesite, the men and women were told to get out. Those too weak or scared to comply were dragged out, kicked and beaten. Then every Jew was ordered to line up at the edge of the ditch and undress. Men, women and children did as they were told, standing naked and shivering, staring down into their own graves. The Germans, with machineguns, then proceeded to shoot the Jews in the back and, one by one, they fell into their graves. The dead, dying and wounded rolling down the dirty slope of the ditch. Bodies stacked like firewood. The soil and the snow mixed with their blood, their human waste and their tears.

Cherna was one of them.

Cherna was a frail woman, who was very religious and who was praying out-loud as the machine-gun fire rang out. She fell face first into the mass grave and rolled straight to the bottom.

While she was laying there with the other bodies, she thought that this was what death was. No heaven, no hell, no golden gates. All she could smell was the powder of spent shells hanging in the air; all she could hear was the sound of other dying Jews weeping into the cold, hard earth as their final breaths escaped their blood-soaked bodies.

When darkness began to fall and the blood from the other bodies started drying on Cherna's arms and legs, she realized that she wasn't dead after all. Miraculously, she was alive! She started to move the arms and legs of dead bodies off her. Freeing herself, she frantically clawed her way, trying to climb out of the grave. A child was crying.

She found the little crying girl, grabbed the child by the hand and helped her over the mound of dead bodies. Naked and covered with the blood of their family and friends, they ran and ran.

They ran until they came to a cottage with a lone candle burning in the window. Scared, cold, naked and hungry, they asked for help. The farmer and his wife gave them a little food and some scraps of old clothing, but told them, "You must go now."

After walking for some time in the dark, cold forest, somehow the little girl and Cherna became separated. Cherna continued on alone for about a week, until she stumbled upon the partisans.

During the slaughter in her town of Kletzk in the winter of 1942, the Germans killed 3,000 men, women and children. Cherna lost her entire family: her husband, four children and nine grandchildren. She was the only survivor. The Germans killed all of the Jews in Kletzk. Kletzk became "Juden Rein" (free of Jews).

---

Sometimes we partisans heard that the Germans were bringing trainloads of Jewish people to the "little green forest" from Hungary, Romania and Czechoslovakia.

I know that this was also the fate of all those doomed souls who had driven past me and my family on the streets of Baranowicze.

As partisans watching tearfully from the sidelines, we were helpless to do anything. As much as we tried and as often as we tried, it was virtually impossible to penetrate the soldiers surrounding the well-guarded area around the mass graves. Some partisans were able to save a few of the Jews who were lucky enough to escape, but not nearly as many as we wanted to.

All we could do was to watch in horror.

# MISSIONS 2: TAKE NO PRISONERS

There were some missions that were more dangerous because the targets weren't buildings or stacks of wood, but living, breathing human beings.

On one of my most dangerous and deadly missions, a group of 5 – a captain, a lieutenant, two of my buddies and myself – were sent to Baranowicze on an assignment of the utmost importance.

It was a mission that would require all the courage and bravery I could muster. A brutal task that would test every one of my skills and push me to my personal limit. Our mission was to "get rid of" two high-ranking German SS officers. In the language of life and death, sometimes the less said the better. Military manuals and articles of war might have used more dignified terms – "assassinate," "execute," "terminate" or "kill" – but we were guerrillas fighting on our own terms.

It was not a game to us, not by any means, but every camp had its own lingo, its own slang, and all of us knew what had to happen in order to "get rid of" anyone, especially deadly SS officers.

Suffice to say these two men were among the elite of the German military. We were each given special guns with silencers and, not one, but two additional grenades in case the mission were to "go sour."

It was a "take-no-prisoners" mission. Kill or be killed. The men we were scheduled to execute not only had both the means and the training to eliminate us, but also the tools to extract all types of information from us if we were to be captured; information that we just could not let them have.

If there ever was a "do or die" mission, this was it.

Our contacts supplied us with clear directions to the house in which the SS officers were living. They also gave us critical information about these officers' movements, their activities, their schedule, their routine. We learned when they arrived and when they left each day, what they did upon leaving, what they did upon returning and pretty much everything in between. This kind of information was crucial to our success.

The location of the house was close to a park not far from the forest, so we only had the dark woods to worry about as we approached the residence of our targets.

One night we went to scope out the house and poke around a bit before taking action. It was spooky, looking at the house where in less than twenty-four hours death and violence would take place.

Whenever we were actually in the presence of the Germans, our fear was always intensified. It was one thing to walk around in the comparative safety of our camp or even talk big on our way to a mission, but to actually be close to a German soldier always sent an icy chill through my veins.

You have to remember that at this time the Germans were still powerful. They were so imposing, so intimidating, so merciless and mighty, that the ground literally shook when they walked. We knew that they cultivated this image, right down to their shiny, black boots and sharp, dark uniforms. Of all the German soldiers, the SS were especially intimidating. (Even, to this day, some sixty years later, whenever I see someone in one of those fashionable black leather coats that stretch down to the knees, the hairs on the back of my neck stand up and I break into in a cold sweat.)

Despite our fears, the next night we went straight to their house. On this mission in particular, the odds were high that the violence would be up-close and personal.

I had never done anything like this.

According to the plan, my buddy and I would dispose of the two guards outside the house. We would creep up and eliminate the two men with our silenced automatics, while a third man backed us up with his rifle from the park. The captain and lieutenant would then sneak inside the house and kill the SS officers at point-blank range with their silenced automatics.

The whole operation took only a few minutes. The SS officers and their guards never knew what hit them. One minute the officers were alive, snoring in their sleep, the next minute they were dead. Dead at the hands of scruffy Jewish and Russian guerrillas, some of them just teenagers.

The moment that I shot the German guard and saw him fall dead to the ground, I knew that I had done a great deed for humanity. I had not killed a human being, I had killed a German soldier. As a partisan I had been involved in many deadly missions that involved killing, but this was different; killing a German soldier close-up gave me a special satisfaction – that of avenging the brutal murders of so many Jews.

This mission afforded me the great pleasure of looking into a German soldier's eyes as I put a bullet in his head, right between his eyes. It had been a long-time desire of mine to kill a German soldier while facing him. Odd, that I am a squeamish person: I cannot look at blood or at a person's injury. It makes me violently sick to my stomach. But killing a German soldier was like killing a mosquito in the Pinsk swamps. As a partisan, I never killed a civilian under any circumstances. I only killed German soldiers.

We owed a lot to our contacts and our scouts. Eternal gratitude for one. They risked their lives to provide us with the information we had just used to terminate four German soldiers. Four soldiers who can no longer cause harm to the Jewish people. Partisan contacts helped us to eliminate many Germans, saving thousands of lives.

---

Not long after assassinating the SS officers, we received good news through our radio operator: The Danes had saved almost all of the Danish Jews from the Germans, more than 7,000 of them.

Hearing that the Germans were planning to round up the Jews and send them to concentration camps, the people and government of Denmark rallied, helping the Jews escape into the night. They smuggled them in small boats, from the shores of Denmark to neutral Sweden, where they were welcomed and kept safe for the remainder of the war. This miracle was due mainly to the efforts of King Christian X of Denmark, who was determined to save his innocent Jewish citizens. As a result, the small community of Danish Jews that had been living among them since the seventeenth century was preserved.

Hearing this extraordinary news from where we were was truly inspiring to those of us in the resistance movement.

The bravery, compassion and humanity of the four-million people of Denmark was in stark contrast to the populations of the other countries occupied by Germany – the Ukraine, Poland, Lithuania, Latvia and Romania – whose citizens helped in the Germans' slaughter of the Jews.

The Lithuanians were just as bad as the Germans. They killed a lot of the Jews from our ghetto in Baranowicze. The Lithuanians, General Wlasof's Ukranian Army and The

Romanian Iron Guard were loyal German "helpers" throughout World War II.

Because of that, we were sent to blow up a small bridge that led to a volunteer Lithuanian military camp and disrupt their activities.

It took three nights to carry out that operation: four of us destroyed this bridge with utmost efficiency.

Now the Lithuanians would have to cross in the water and carry their weapons and supplies on their shoulders. This would slow them down, hampering their progress on the way to kill more of my people.

Life was becoming tough for the Germans because they knew they were losing on the Eastern front. And now they couldn't even control a hearty band of partisans in the forest.

---

One day Genia, my buddy Mishka and I were sent on a mission to get information from a contact concerning heavy truck movement in the east; information that was very important to the Russian army. It would then be transmitted by radio to Moscow and used by the generals fighting the war.

I was very nervous and concerned for Genia's safety. Since I was taller, weighed 180 pounds and she weighed only 100 pounds, I told Genia to walk behind me and "to stay in my shadow."

The trip was without incident. We rendezvoused with our contact, received the vital information and started walking back to camp.

All of a sudden we stumbled upon a group of German soldiers walking on the road in front of us. By the time we saw them, they had already seen our shadows, gotten scared and started shooting at us.

As I turned to run, I was shot in my right hip. I could have gone down, but the fear of dying far outweighed any pain. So I kept running, at first without even limping. Somehow my adrenaline drove me and I was able to run for awhile longer. Then, with the help of Genia and Mishka, I slowly limped my way back to camp.

It was a miracle that the bullet did not shatter my hipbone, it simply went right through my flesh.

---

In the partisan camps, however, there was no time to rest. As soon as my hip healed, which took a little over a month, I was working again. After having already added bombardier, wire cutter, explosives expert and assassin to my guerrilla résumé, I was going to add yet another: spy.

This time, four of us were being sent to a nearby partisan brigade by the name of Zorkincy, which was made up of all gentiles. We were sent to investigate rumors of Jewish civilians being murdered by this group of partisans. It alarmed us all to no end to think that other partisans, our comrades, were killing the Jews just like the Germans. It was an extremely dangerous mission. Since some of us could always pass for gentiles, we were carefully selected. I was proud to go.

In the Zorkincy camp we were assigned to the kitchen to peel potatoes, chop wood and keep night watch. We performed our duties efficiently, taking in our surroundings, asking questions and gathering all the information the unsuspecting gentile partisans could provide.

They did not know that we were Jewish. They only knew and cared that we were young and strong. They thought we were just young kids, what the heck did we know? Let us peel potatoes, start some fires. And so we did.

We stayed there for about a month, gathering confidential information. When we got back to camp, Colonel Niecolski listened carefully to our report, writing down various pieces of information that we provided – names, times, dates, evidence and clues.

We told the colonel that we felt dirty living among people we suspected of killing our Jewish brothers, but our commandant assured us that our time was well spent, and absolutely necessary.

# PARTISAN WEDDING - LOVE IN THE FOREST

All was not death and destruction. Away from the doomed ghettos, away from the deadly German front lines of the Russian border, buried deep within the confines of our secluded swamp, there was time between one fellow partisan and another for the occasional smile, the laugh, the cigarette, the whisper, the wink, the nudge, or the hug.

There was even time for a partisan wedding.

As February drew to a close, I felt myself yearning for more time with Genia. Not just fireside time in the evenings, but daytime as well. Breakfast time. Lunch time. Dinner time. All of my time.

After I returned from my spying assignment, I decided that it was the right time for me to propose to Genia – and if she said yes, we would get married. But I did not know how to approach it. I had to wait for the right moment.

One evening that moment became a reality. It had been too cold to remain outdoors so we had moved from the campfire back to my bunk. Genia had just sang a beautiful song and was sitting next to me. I was still too shy to take her hand, but she took mine in hers and, as we talked, brought it to her mouth for a slow, tender kiss, remarking that I had beautiful hands. Well *that* sent a jolt of electricity shooting through my young body.

I knew all-too-well that a partisan's life was short. If I didn't ask her now, would there be another day? Did any of us ever know when the todays might end and the tomorrows stop coming?

I didn't have a right, but in the small, cramped bunk I was already on my knees and, so with courage, simply asked Genia, "Would you like to change your last name to Lato?"

To my surprise, Genia said yes without hesitation.

It was February 23, 1944.

The next morning after breakfast, February 24, I asked Genia's father Judel for her hand in marriage. It was like proposing all over again. I waited anxiously. His smile of pride and satisfaction were answer enough, but he went on to hug and kiss me before he answered yes.

Later that morning, Judel said a prayer and married us in a simple ceremony with some of our friends as witnesses. It was a rare and happy time for joy, love and passion and, above all, hope amid the misery and heartache of most other forest days. We sang, played music, drank some vodka and that was that. Then we went back to our duties.

The bunks were a crowded place and there was no such thing as "a partisan honeymoon." With up to 30 other people sharing "our" bunk, not to mention her father and brother sleeping right next to us, there was no monkey business for the happy couple that night, nor for many nights to come.

But we didn't care. We were blessed. We had found love, friendship and joy during wartime. We had found each other.

Eventually Genia and I were assigned to a different brigade, the "Grysodubow *otriad*." My wife tended to sick or wounded partisans. She was very nurturing, quite good at compassionate care and had a knack for making the sick feel better.

I was assigned to a civilian paratrooper as his personal companion. He was a very intelligent gentleman who spoke fluent Polish, Russian and German. We would go out on missions about two or three times a month. In-between I had time with Genia.

Since we did all of our traveling at night, we used to rest during the day. When I traveled with the civilian paratrooper, I was sworn to complete secrecy. Whoever we met, wherever we went, I had to keep it to myself. I couldn't even tell my wife. We traveled all over the region and he met with a lot of different people. Some of the meetings lasted a long time and seemed very important. While the paratrooper was in meetings, I stayed outside. I was instructed not to ask questions about where we were going or what we were doing. We did have long conversations about the war – about Hitler, Roosevelt, Churchill and Stalin – the mistakes made by the world in allowing Hitler to come into power, the Jewish situation and anything else that came to mind. He was a kind and generous man and never made me feel less important than he was.

We were together for about ten weeks. Then he left the forest and returned to Mother Russia.

During that time I had no idea who that paratrooper was or exactly what he was doing during those clandestine meetings. Only after he left was I told that he was the Polish Prime Minister Designate, organizing the Polish government for the eventual liberation. I never did find out his name. I always called him "Pan," which in Polish means sir.

In meeting, befriending, serving and fighting with people like Captain Misha, General Orlowsky and the Polish Prime

Minister Designate, I managed not just to survive, but to *live*.

# LIBERATION

*July 22, 1944*

The war was changing overnight. In our area of the Polesie swamps, liberation was fast approaching, although the war in Western Europe had not yet started.

After the civilian paratrooper left, Genia and I were transferred back to our old group of paratroopers. The main mission from then on – until liberation itself – remained the same: to kill as many German soldiers as possible.

The paratroopers' mission had evolved. We were more active, more confrontational. Better armed, better equipped and better trained, we made better use of our talents and took our guerrilla war straight to the Germans.

We would travel by night to the houses in which the German soldiers lived and firebomb or throw grenades into their living quarters.

These were grim and serious missions and, we believed, vital to turning the tide of the war.

---

In the spring of 1944, a ghetto survivor somehow managed to stumble into our partisan camp. It was then that I learned the tragic story of my father's death.

In March 1943 the group of 127 people in the labor camp for tradesmen decided to dig an escape tunnel under the camp. They started digging underneath the bunker where they lived and continued until they reached the outside beyond the barbed and electric wire that surrounded the camp. They used tablespoons to dig the tunnel at night, the same as we had dug the tunnel under our house in the ghetto of Baranowicze. In the morning they put the dirt in their pockets and got rid of it on their way to work. It took them over a year to complete this vast undertaking.

Once the tunnel was finished, they picked a night – Passover Eve, 1st Seder – to make their break. Before escaping, the 127 drew straws to decide who would be the one to stay behind. That doomed person would have to camouflage the escape route after the other 12 had fled. This would give them a head start before being discovered. Without a doubt, that person would surely be killed – it was a suicide mission of the highest order. But the price had to be paid to save the others.

On the night of the escape, it was very dark, perhaps too dark. But the escapees knew that they had no choice, they had to run away. Because of the darkness, they got lost in the field outside the camp. Then, in all the confusion, they got separated into three groups. My father's group of 27 was caught by the Germans, who brought them all back to the camp and killed them.

The other two groups managed to escape. After days of searching, they finally found several partisan camps. A few of them, including the man who was telling the story, wound up in our camp. When he said that my father had been killed on Passover, the moment I heard that I silently vowed, in memory of my father, never again to take bread on Passover.

---

In June of 1944 shortly before liberation, news reached camp that my mother Sara and my little brother Jackob had been killed on Christmas 1943.

They had been at the brick factory for a year. One night when they returned from work, they were all taken from the labor camp and placed in the back of trucks with vents specifically installed to deliver a lethal dose of poisonous Zyklon-B gas. Efficiently and speedily, this gas would kill the Jews while they were being transported to their mass graves.

The German butchers finally murdered the remaining 235 Jews from the brick factory in Baranowicze.

My town was now irrevocably *"Juden Rein,"* free of Jews.

Now my mother and my brother were gone, too.

They were all gone.

Except me.

---

American forces crossed the channels on June 7, 1944. Our operations continued until we were liberated by the Russian army on July 22, 1944.

That day was a holiday and the excitement and celebration did not stop until very late that night.

For the partisans in the Polesie swamps, the guerrilla war had finally ended. But for those of us who were recruited into the Russian army, the war was just beginning.

The Russian military recruited 127 men from our brigade, including myself and my brother-in-law. We said tearful goodbyes to our partisan comrades not knowing if we would ever see them again.

There was little time for contemplation between the two wars I would fight during World War II.

I officially became a Russian solder in July 1944 and joined a regiment about twenty miles away near Bialystok, Poland, and began fighting right away. It was a continuation of my war against the Germans.

The only difference was that I was wearing a better uniform.

**LEFT**
Genia Wishnia Lato, Baranowicze 1938. Genia and I were married in the Partisan camp on February 24, 1944.

**ABOVE**
July 23, 1944, me one day after liberation by the Russian army. Picture taken in the Lipiczany Forest.

**RIGHT**
Genia and me a few days after I signed up for the Russian army, Baranowicze 1944.

# Part 5
# The Russian Army

"May it be His will to renew for us a good and sweet year"

– Traditional Rosh Hashanah prayer

# THE RUSSIAN FRONT

After walking for two days, we reached the Russian front around 10 p.m. We were inducted upon arrival. We were introduced to our battalion commander, our company and our platoons. The kitchen gave us a loaf of white bread and a large cup of potato soup. I polished it off immediately. It tasted exceptionally good. I hadn't eaten food like that for over three years, since before the war.

That night they officially assigned us to the battalion. This one consisted of 800 to 1,000 men. I got to keep my automatic rifle (my "P.P. Sha"), which had a 72-bullet magazine, my revolver and three grenades. The captain gave us instructions about future offensive attacks and taught us how to break through the German defensive lines. By the time we went to sleep it was midnight.

Next day they woke us at 5 a.m. Again we were given a slice of bread, a cup of potato soup and a big glass of vodka. We were to stay ready to start the attack against the German trenches. The signal would be a green flare. Once we see the flare, we were to go forward in the direction of the trenches, running and screaming whatever comes to mind. At 6 a.m. Russian artillery started shelling German positions. It lasted for almost two hours. During the bombardment I realized that very few Germans could survive this attack. The Russian artillery was murderous. No wonder the Russians called their artillery "The Mother of War."

At 8 a.m. the green rocket flare went up and we moved forward. We did not encounter too much resistance in the beginning of the attack. We crossed trenches loaded with dead or wounded German soldiers. We moved with success for about three miles. A lot of German soldiers ran away from their lines. While I was running full speed, screaming "victory for Mother

Russia," "revenge for the Jewish lives," "victory" and "revenge," all of a sudden I heard the sound of a German artillery shell coming in my direction. To avoid collision with the shell – and instant death – I immediately hit the ground. The shell hit the ground at the same time as I did. I felt the impact. I was still alive, afraid to move. Afraid to move even a finger in case it would create a wave. Very slowly I lifted my head and looked: the shell was lying three feet away from me. It had *not* exploded! I asked myself, Is this really happening to me on the first day I joined the army? The artillery shell was lying there next to me: silently and motionless, just like me. Shocked and dazed, I stared at the shell in disbelief. I had been spared again.

That first day of combat, we lost 120 men of the original 127 partisans recruited by the Russians. Only seven of us survived, and I was one of the lucky ones. My wife's brother was among the wounded. Our 127 partisans were like brothers. We had fought together as guerrilla fighters in the Belarus forest against the Germans, but we had never been trained in military tactics. Lack of experience in open field military warfare was one of the reasons that our group suffered the most casualties. We were also the first unit to reach the German resistance and took a heavy shelling from German artillery.

The following day we learned that the offensive was successful. The Russians had destroyed the Germans first and second lines of defense and moved westward about twelve miles, then settled there for awhile until the supply lines caught up. Meanwhile the front line – the Russians' first line of defense – had been established.

The seven who survived were pulled back over a mile to the rear of the front to wait for the army to regroup our battalion.

Slowly replacement soldiers started to arrive. On the seventh day we received a group of about 120 men. I recognized some of them from our area of the forest; some from Baranowicze.

The commander assigned three of us, myself and two sergeants, to a machine-gun platoon to deliver food, supplies and ammunition to our soldiers in the trenches and foxholes at the front.

Once our battalion and platoon were filled with new soldiers, the commander informed us that we would be moving to the front line in two days.

For the next two days we prepared for a new offensive. Again the artillery would shell the German trenches for two hours, from 6 to 8 a.m., and then the infantry would go forward on attack.

Our machine-gun platoon had 10 heavy, water-cooled machine guns on wheels, four men to each gun. There were four platoons to a company and five or six companies to a battalion. There were four lieutenants, one for each platoon; one captain for each company and one colonel for the battalion.

My company stayed about five hundred yards behind the infantry until the new front line was established. The machine guns were placed in certain areas, usually on higher ground, to create the first line of defense. They were also placed in special foxholes to protect them. Many times they were moved to confuse the enemy.

Our job was to deliver supplies directly to the front line to our platoon five or six times a day and, if necessary, water for the cooling systems for the machine guns. It was a dangerous assignment, but it was better than sitting in the trenches. We did not use trucks or jeeps. On the front line we did mostly everything on foot and sometimes used horses and wagons because they were quieter than trucks.

One day during that combat, I was sitting having lunch with my two sergeants when we saw a German plane hit by anti-aircraft artillery. We saw smoke coming from the plane and then realized that it was going down and coming directly at us. We got up and ran. We saw a foxhole and jumped in. The plane hit the ground about seventy yards from us and exploded. It must have been loaded with bombs because the explosion was so powerful that it turned over our wagons and our horses. The horses went completely wild. It was so loud that we all lost our hearing for a couple days. When we went to investigate we found a very large crater where the plane hit but no sign of the plane. It had completely disintegrated. I had been lucky again.

Two days later the shelling of German positions began again. The Russian artillery delivered *katyusha* rockets, which were devastating. It lasted two hours. Then the infantry received the order to attack. Many Germans were killed, wounded or just ran away. The next six miles were easy until the Germans regrouped. Once the Germans started to put up resistance, the infantry stopped and established a front.

Every trip to and from the front line was hard physically and treacherous. The supplies were heavy and had to be carried on our shoulders. Many times when we were walking, German snipers tried to pick us off and we dropped to the ground and crawled on our bellies.

During the six weeks I served on this assignment, one of my sergeants was killed and one was seriously wounded.

From time to time soldiers in the trenches or in foxholes lost men to snipers or from direct hits by artillery shells. These men were immediately replaced with new soldiers.

Those first six weeks in the army became routine - deliver, come back, fill the pack and deliver again, every three to four hours. The distance between our station and the front line was about a half of a mile, but it took us a long time to walk it. The grounds were flat and had few trees or shrubs for cover.

Every so often the Russians advanced the front line and the machine-gun platoons went with them.

About a month after our first offensive I noticed that our

battalion had not taken any German soldiers prisoners of war. I asked around and was told by the Russian soldiers that they were killing them off. The Russians hated the Germans as much as the Jews did. The Germans had inflicted a lot of suffering and casualties on Russian civilian populations. When the Russian command learned that their soldiers were killing the German prisoners, they ordered them to stop or face severe penalties: courts-marital, perhaps, the firing squad.

After the offensive, two Polish officers approached me from the Polish People's Army, which was under Russian supervision, and offered me a commission if I were willing to become an officer in the Polish army. I thanked them, but turned them down. I told them that I was Jewish and would rather be with the Russian army. Then I apologized for expressing my feelings and told them I appreciated their interest in me.

---

In mid-September 1944 our company moved back from the front line for a little break, what we called a "short vacation," then moved north to join another battalion. The Russians told us this was in preparation for a major offensive, the big push to the East Prussian capital of Konigsberg, part of Germany and north of Poland and south of the Baltic Sea.

One day a captain ordered me to follow him. He was taking me to see the colonel. I was worried. What did he want with me? The colonel asked me if I wanted to be part of the battalion bookkeepers group. They had checked my educational background and felt that I was capable. Even more, they had asked me, not ordered me. I accepted the assignment and thanked the colonel. I reported directly to him.

With that I moved from the machine-gun platoon to the bookkeeping squad, which was much safer. We were over a mile from the front line. The food was a little better, cleaner; I could sleep under a roof, not in a trench, and mingle with officers.

I kept the bookkeeping position for almost six weeks, which is a long time in the army. It was during this time that I started to be concerned with surviving the war. There had been a lot of close calls. I was tired of risking my life. The war's end wasn't far away and I was thinking about my wife Genia a lot. I missed her. I knew she was fine and I was sure that she still loved me and remembered me. I wrote her letters every day and I received some from her often, though it took a long time to get them. Genia had written that a few weeks after I had left for the Russian front, she and her father Judel returned to Baranowicze. Judel found work as manager of a lumberyard whose owner was killed during the Holocaust. Genia got a very prestigious job: she was personal secretary to the Attorney General of Baranowicze province. Judel and Genia continued their rescue work, saving Jews from being deported to Siberia and smuggling them to Poland. Judel had been chosen to be the leader of the survivors. He was like a surrogate father, providing legal and practical advice to survivors and helping them find jobs.

Waiting to start the big push to Konigsberg, I thought a lot about Genia.

---

In early October I contracted what they called a very rare infection, "Rose Poison," in my right arm and had to undergo surgery immediately. I was in the hospital for nine days, then sent to a Health Battalion two miles from the front line for another two weeks. While there I accepted an unusual assignment: to give lectures to Russian soldiers on different countries, political systems and current affairs.

While I was recuperating the captain gave me a form to fill

out to apply to the prestigious Russian Aviation School in Moscow. They would choose only three applicants, one from each battalion. That same day, I was picked. The following day, they took me to regiment headquarters to be interviewed and tested. The tests included Russian language, geography, physics, chemistry, math and geometry. I had been a good student so I had no problem with the evaluations. Then I was interviewed by the general, who hinted that I had scored well. He asked my nationality. When I said "Jewish," the tone of his voice changed. He asked me to wait in another room. Shortly after, another captain came in to tell me that the positions had already been filled; instead they would send me to officer's school for three months to become a lieutenant. I wasn't fooled. I understood what had happened.

I was rejected because I was a Jew. My pride was hurt. To be rejected because of my nationality was the worst disappointment and gave me a bad feeling. This was the first anti-Semitic incident that happened to me in the army. I realized that the general was a Jew hater. I didn't want to attend officer's school. I didn't want to be a lieutenant in the Russian army. Being a lieutenant was the most dangerous position on the front line. I wanted to survive the war.

I preferred to be a plain soldier.

My arm healed without complications and I rejoined my assigned group at battalion headquarters and began to deliver lectures to soldiers who were on leisure time and to wounded soldiers who were recuperating. Officially I was a political adviser to the colonel.

I told stories about my life in the ghetto, about German soldiers killing the Jews, about my life as a partisan, about my life in Poland and about life in other countries. I spent a lot of time with the colonel. We had discussions about Hitler, Churchill, Roosevelt, we talked about history, fascism, communism, capitalism and hatred. The colonel hated the Germans almost as much as I did. He wanted to know about the Holocaust and the partisans and I told him all about it. I was only nineteen years old but he respected me and treated me as an equal even though he was thirty-five years old. I had some kind of magnetism, attracting people who liked me, took an interest in me, respected me and helped make my life more pleasant.

While we were waiting for the big push, the big offense, the colonel sent me to visit soldiers in foxholes and in field hospitals. He wanted to know about their conditions, if they were getting their food deliveries. He wanted to help them keep up their morale. I asked them what they thought about the offensive, about Hitler and the German army. I reported all their comments to the colonel.

Early one morning we are awakened by loud explosions. The Germans were trying to break through our front line. Their artillery shelled our positions for a while, but didn't do much damage. After the shelling, their infantry started a ground attack. Our heavy machine-gun units repelled them at first and the Germans retreated back to their trenches. They regrouped and tried again without success. They suffered a lot of casualties. Meanwhile the Russian command moved its artillery closer to prepare for another attack.

The Germans attacked again. This time they used tanks and the infantry followed behind. They tried to break down our first line of defense, but the Russian anti-tank artillery was stronger. It did not take long for the Russians to silence them. Finally the Germans gave up and retreated for good. They lost many tanks and a large number of soldiers. Our battalion suffered casualties, but we had held the line. After the battle was over, the colonel went to the front line to congratulate the soldiers for their bravery.

We were close to East Prussia and knew that we were

nearing a major offensive. We didn't know how large and powerful the German army was at this point, but we were sure that it would take a very strong fight to defeat them in battle.

I happened to stop at an individual foxhole with one soldier in it. He was an older man with a goatee and a mustache. He reminded me of my grandfather. I introduced myself. I found out that he was a rabbi, a Holocaust survivor and had been a partisan somewhere north of Baranowicze. He told me that he was the only survivor in *his* family. When he learned that I also was Jewish, a sole survivor and a partisan, he asked me if I could help him get re-assigned to another company, away from the trenches. After surviving all he had, he feared that he was going to be killed in a foxhole on the front line.

I felt sorry for this man and ran to headquarters with his story, begging the colonel to help this fifty-five-year-old pious man. The colonel gave me permission to go pick him up and bring him in. I ran as fast as I could back to the front, almost getting killed by a sniper's bullet. I found the foxhole and started to tell him that he was being pulled from the trenches when I suddenly realized that he was already dead. I was too late. I felt as if I had lost a close friend.

When I returned and reported this to the colonel, he remarked, "We tried. It was not meant for us to save him."

# THE BIG PUSH

One afternoon when I was walking on flat land to the front line with two other sergeants, the Germans dropped a few artillery shells in our direction. We kept on going until their sharpshooters pinned us down. We were in the open and could not move; could not improve our position by crawling. Every time one of us moved, a bullet hit close by. A bullet grazed my left arm, but it wasn't serious. We waited about three or four hours until dark, then crawled to safety. We survived the ordeal even though our positions were on flat land without cover. They were lousy sharpshooters. Why? Because at that point the German army was recruiting inexperienced soldiers, young kids and older men. They were not the invincible, unbeatable, powerful force that they had been in the beginning when they started the war. They were an ordinary bunch of weak soldiers, with little or no experience. But they hated the Russians and the Jews just the same.

At the end of January 1945 I observed a lot of movement in our area. Trucks passed pulling large amounts of artillery units, a lot of *katyushas*, and more soldiers, officers, supplies and convoys.

More horses and wagons were brought to our battalion. We assumed the big attack was coming. We asked questions, but got no answers. The officers were uncommonly quiet. There was a complete blackout of normal communications. Everything was confidential. We were told to sit, to wait for "orders" and keep our morale up.

Then one day, we were awakened at 4 a.m., fed breakfast and told to be ready. An hour later Russian artillery started shelling German positions all along the Northern front. The shelling was devastatingly awesome. It's impossible to describe or even imagine the power of it. The noise made it sound like I was inside of a grinding machine. I couldn't imagine anyone surviving shelling like this. I could feel the ground shaking under my feet. It was really scary. The sky was red from fire. The shelling went on for hours. It reminded me of the things that I had heard about the Stalingrad offensive, when the German army surrendered and the Russian army captured 300,000 German POWs I believe the Russian army probably had assembled the same kind of power here.

Finally, slowly, the shelling stopped and our regiment received the order to move forward. Our headquarters went, too. We crossed the Polish border into East Prussia and continued moving with very little resistance, just small pockets of opposition. By then we were in German territory and the destruction all around us was surreal. Everything was destroyed. We kept walking until dark, we'd covered twenty miles when headquarters decided to stop. The German defense had completely collapsed. The infantry continued to go forward to establish a front line almost twenty miles farther north.

The next day we moved north to get closer to our regiment. The German army at the front was in complete disarray. Our infantry had captured a lot of POWs. We still had not seen any German civilians; they were still hiding. The infantry was moving slowly north, establishing new lines along the way. A few days later we reached the town of Gutstadt and the commander made his headquarters there. The infantry went a few miles farther north, established a front line and waited until the army regrouped for the final push to victory in that region.

This major offensive lasted for two weeks. Then the Russian artillery units, needed somewhere else, suddenly disappeared. All the equipment went with them, too. Our battalion had accomplished its job. We had cut the German army in our region off from their central forces in the west in the heart of Germany. The Russian Second Army encircled the German army, which we had fought, and destroyed it.

In Gutstadt we were assigned to a large bank building and an adjoining building for headquarters. I was lucky again. I was staying with the big wigs. The army opened the vaults and took out everything. They only left the German currency, the marks, which by then were worthless. Still, many soldiers started to pack large bags of money to keep. We used the money to start fires in the ovens to warm the building. It was wintertime and extremely cold.

I was just counting the days to the end of the killing.

I stayed with the officers at headquarters, lecturing 75 to 100 soldiers at a time under the cover of a closed building. I also visited troops in the trenches at the front line. I was allowed to ride a horse-drawn wagon, but was told to be careful and not to go into town. We discovered a long freight train loaded with canned foods. We sampled the food carefully to make sure it wasn't poisoned. It was okay. The soldiers stampeded the train. It was enough food to feed a whole army. We snacked all day long. When the army finally opened the town, a group went just to see how the rich people there had lived. The Russians were amazed by the capitalist life and asked me a lot of questions.

In one of the houses, on a couch in the parlor, we found two dead bodies. A man and a woman, a young couple; both naked. The man was on top of the woman in the act of lovemaking. They were shot with one bullet, and there was a bayonet pierced through both of their bodies. We assumed that some Russian soldiers killed them in revenge. We reported it to the authorities.

In the meantime, more civilians started coming into the streets. The army issued orders to the military to respect the German homes that still existed and to be careful not to get involved with the civilians, to avoid arguments with them. Anybody breaking this law would receive a courts-martial.

Many times the army tried to move the front line farther forward to improve its position and make a more formidable first line to defend. However the army was short of men. So, from time to time, some of us were assigned to fill the gap. The command did not want to disturb the men in the trenches on the front line.

One day seven of us were ordered to take and occupy an empty house located on a little hill on our right flank. It was a good location for forward observations. Weather conditions were very bad. The command ordered a few platoons to cover our left flank.

As we moved toward the house machinegun and rifle fire broke out. We were under attack. German soldiers and sharpshooters were in the house. In the surprise and confusion, we jumped into a creek with running water in front of us.

It was ice cold. We were trapped, pinned down by a few snipers and machine guns. The territory was flat, no trees, no shrubs or other places for cover. If we ran to the house they would pick us off one by one. We had to wait in freezing water. It was February 1945. I dropped down into the water on my stomach behind a small a rock and tried to stay behind it. Every once in a while a sniper's bullet would hit the back of my heavy, bulky winter coat and I would feel the ripple. Every time somebody tried to move, they were hit.

It seemed like hours before we heard artillery shells going off. Then a few shells hit the house. When the smoke cleared, we trudged stiffly out of the creek and up to what remained of the house. We found seven Germans inside, five dead and two injured, but alive. We delivered the POWs to our command.

When I took off my heavy coat, I saw it had bullet holes in the back. I counted eleven of them. They had all missed.

---

Now the Russians began talking about finishing off the German army in Eastern Prussia. Because the army was short of troops, they were going to send everyone. I got worried. I really did not want to go to the front and sit in a foxhole and do the shooting. I had had enough shooting in my short lifetime.

They started moving regiments to the Western front. Rumors were we were moving soon.

But the colonel surprised me with a temporary job in the field hospital next to headquarters. I worked there for one day. The job was an orderly in the operating room. As soon as the doctor handed me an amputated leg to dispose of I got sick to my stomach. I knew the colonel wanted me to be safe, but I could not stay there.

I went back to the colonel. He told me that sooner or later we'd all be sent to the front lines, except for the medical staff. I had a funny feeling that the colonel knew about my life, and that is why he wanted to protect me. He had told me once that he thought that I had a great future. He knew that something serious was going to happen because our division, after all the casualties, didn't have enough manpower or equipment. Even worse, we were six or seven miles from the Baltic Sea, the site of the last attack and where we needed to reach to end the big offensive. I suspected that the colonel was not sure that we were going to make it.

It was life or death for the Germans.

It was life or death for all of us.

# DODGING A FINAL BULLET

March 3, 1945. It would have been my brother's twelfth birthday, one week after my own twentieth birthday. At breakfast the day became even more memorable, if this was possible. This was the day we were given our attack instructions.

They said: "We will go after the artillery stops shelling the German positions. We will form one line of soldiers, each man about fifty feet from the other. The line will consist of officers, soldiers and everyone and anybody else available. When you see the green flare, we go on attack. Then everyone is on his own until we reach the Baltic Sea."

---

I was running like everybody else, my automatic rifle ready to shoot, without encountering any noticeable resistance. I stopped to catch my breath. Suddenly 3 Russian soldiers asked me where I was going. I said, I was going to the Baltic Sea. They drew their pistols and, in German, ordered me to put my arms up and surrender. I reacted instinctively, squeezing the trigger and firing my automatic rifle until the three of them had fallen to the ground, splashing the snow with their blood. But I was down, too. One of them had managed to put a bullet in my gut. They were lying dead in the snow, with blood all around them. I was still conscious. Somehow, I had not lost consciousness. I filled my helmet with snow and put it on my head. I wanted to control my senses and my brain after a bullet had exploded in the middle of my body.

In the army you learned that if someone is wounded in the belly, he usually dies within five hours unless he has surgery. I needed to get myself to the road where someone could see me.

My army buddy, Kruwcow, on my right flank, heard the shots and came over to look for me. He found me crawling in snow in the direction of the nearest road, blood in my mouth and nose. The clothes on my belly and part of my chest in shambles, soaked with blood. I was murmuring over and over, "Mama, I am coming to join you. Mama, I am coming to join you."

Kruwcow pulled me to the road just as a Russian soldier on a horse and sled was passing by. He stopped, they put me on the sled and took me to a makeshift field hospital, a former school in Gutstadt. My good luck was with me again. I was still alert, but scared that this time I was going to die.

The Russian doctors operated immediately, without anesthesia, using only a freezing injection, which they had applied on my belly because my right lung was open. The doctors talked to me during the surgery. The bullet had exploded between my rib cage and my belly. It smashed four ribs, bore a hole in my right lung and ruptured some arteries, causing some minor damage to my liver. Miraculously, my mother's letter, which I always carried in a leather pouch around my neck, had shifted to my left side and was untouched.

I felt that my guardian angel was still watching over me and had saved my life again.

I was in intensive care for two weeks, and then transferred to a hospital in Konigsberg, where I received excellent care from the Russian military doctors, most of whom were women. I was there another two weeks, and then transferred again, this time to a hospital in Kovno, the capital of Lithuania, where, except for the doctors, the medical staff was primarily civilian. I found most of the personnel there anti-Semitic.

In my treatment, the doctors connected a hose to my abdomen and there was a bottle hanging from my shoulder to below my waistline to collect my body fluids. These connections needed to be attended every day in the operating room by a doctor. The healing process was projected to last between four and five months.

Soon after I was transferred again, this time to Minsk, the capital of Belarus. Upon arrival I was put in the operating room to be examined by a doctor. While lying there, an elderly lady came in, walked around the room and after a few minutes came over and asked me in a whisper if I was Jewish. I said yes. She told me that she was the doctor assigned to me and that she was also Jewish. She asked me if I was a survivor of the ghetto. When I said I was, she asked me to tell her about it. While she changed the bottles, cleaned and bandaged my wound, I told her about my experiences in the ghetto.

In this hospital I received help with my walking. I had not walked for almost six weeks. The doctors in the other hospitals had kept me in bed. Here I started to walk and move around. This was thanks to the charge nurse who had devised the contraption to hold the bottle that was hanging from my shoulder. She used to bring me extra food, milk, slices of bread and soup. I would exchange cigarettes and tobacco with my roommates for their desserts, compotes or ice cream.

The people were very pleasant and very polite. I liked this place. I started writing beautiful love letters to my Genia. I told her of my progress, how much I missed her and wanted to see her. I also had time to read a lot. The doctor was kind enough to bring books for me to read in Russian, German, Polish and Yiddish.

But as soon as I got settled in, it happened again: I was transferred to still another hospital. This one in Ryazan, two hundred miles east of Moscow and one thousand miles away from where I was.

The medics put me in an ambulance and took me to the train station. There they moved me into the Red Cross car for wounded soldiers and told me that for me "the war was over." It was the end of April 1945.

On the way to Ryazan, over the course of five hundred miles from Minsk to Smolensk, I saw devastation all over the landscape. I saw women working the land and rebuilding houses that had been destroyed by the Germans. I saw burned towns and villages and very little animal life. It was really depressing.

At the station in Ryazan, an ambulance was waiting to take us to the hospital.

I had to share a room with 19 men, all of them Russian soldiers. When I was taken for a bath, I got a surprise treat when two female nurses came in, undressed and took a hot bath right in front of me. When they finished, they got dressed as if no one was there and left. My nurse told me that it was a normal routine; nurses did not have access to hot baths in their apartments, so they bathed at work.

That same day I had two women visitors after dinner. Katia and Olga, who worked in a nearby factory, were volunteers who came to the hospital on alternate days to help us keep our morale up. They brought me books from the library.

---

The first day of May was the big Russian holiday and the town had a big celebration, with parades and everything. I felt excitement in the air. Everybody was talking about how the war was going to end soon. I read in the newspaper that Hitler and his girlfriend, Eva Braun, were hiding somewhere in Berlin in underground bunkers. The German army was completely destroyed. Everybody knew that the fighting was over, but officially the war was not over because the German army had not yet surrendered.

I missed Genia. I had not seen her for almost a year. I wrote to her almost every day, but I only received letters from her in bunches. Russian mail to soldiers accumulated and was censored. I knew my wife's letters had been read because some of the sentences were blacked out.

It didn't stop me from reading them over and over again.

# END OF WAR, BUT NOT PREJUDICE

On May 8, 1945, it was announced over the hospital loudspeakers that the German government had surrendered. The war was officially over!

Everybody in the room went crazy. Soldiers who could not walk started to dance and sing. I broke down and cried. I had survived the hell, but my family had not. It was an emotional time. I settled down after a while and celebrated the German defeat with my fellow patients. People everywhere were shouting "The war is over! The war is over!" That's all I would hear for over a day.

The hospital gave us permission to join the people on the street. The fellow in the next bed, on crutches himself, helped me walk outside to feel the vibration and excitement. I was amazed by the celebration. Everything was closed. Nobody went to work. Strangers were dancing, singing and hugging each other. I could not believe what I was watching. I could never have imagined it. The war had lasted over four years and Russia had suffered millions of casualties at the hands of the Germans. Peace in the world was welcomed.

I read in the newspaper that Hitler and Eva Braun were found dead in their bunker in Berlin. They had committed suicide. The rest of the big German authorities – Goerring, Himmler, Ribentrop and many of the others – surrendered to the allies. (Later they would face the International Tribunal in Nuremberg, Germany, and be convicted of war crimes.)

After all the celebrations quieted down, I went back to my everyday routine, which was very simple. My big activity each day was to see the doctor in the operating room and have my wound cleaned and my bottle changed. It had been a little over two months with the wound. After those visits, I would read my books, the newspapers, write love letters to my wife, then eat and take a nap. In the evenings, I waited for visitors, the volunteers, and we talked about what had happened to me in the ghetto. Some times, listening to my stories, the volunteers cried. Some of them had lost family during the war, too.

Mostly, I spent my days waiting and waiting, hoping to feel better, improve enough to be able to go home to my wife and my new family. This was how I spent my time: waiting for my wound to heal.

---

In early June 1945, I overheard a conversation. Some men were talking: one soldier, who had lost both legs in battle, was saying, "Hitler was a very smart man, a great and powerful leader who made the big mistake of leaving some Jewish people alive."

I couldn't believe what I was hearing and flipped out, and went to confront him. In a very loud voice I told him that I was Jewish and that he didn't know the difference between a Jew and a gentile. I started screaming at him, calling him all kinds of names. I was lucky I was too weak; otherwise I might have killed him. I cursed him out and told him that I would report this to the military authority. He apologized for "not knowing that I was Jewish." I gave him a lecture. I told him that what really mattered was that he was a Jew hater.

I went right to the commandant and reported the incident. I requested that he move this soldier out of my room.

A few hours later, two soldiers arrived in our room with a wheelchair. They were there for that soldier. They put the Jew hater in the wheelchair and moved him out. No questions asked.

Everybody felt relieved and praised me for the way that I handled it.

After that incident, I never heard any other remarks about Jews.

# HOMEWARD BOUND

A day came when I was instructed to go the commandant's office. Someone was there waiting for me. I could not imagine who it could be. I was a thousand miles from Baranowicze and knew no one here.

When I walked in I thought I was dreaming! It was my beautiful wife Genia before me. We hugged and hugged, wordlessly. We cried from happiness. After the shock wore off, we told each other how much we loved each other.

The hospital commandant was amazed that my wife had even found me.

Genia had come for me. I still had an open wound and the bottle hanging on my side, but I was going home. Finally!

The general in charge of all the military hospitals had told Genia that he felt I would heal faster at home, in her care. He even had the necessary documents ready.

After my lady doctor carefully instructed my wife on the care I would require, she hugged Genia, praised her energy and bravery, then said goodbye to me.

We would travel to Moscow, stay there a few days until we obtained a permit to go to Baranowicze and then head for our beloved home.

My army days were over. My partisan days were over. My ghetto days were over. The German army was destroyed. The Jews had paid an unbearably heavy price.

I was twenty. My wife and I were finally together. One day we would have our honeymoon. We did not know our destiny, but together we had a future to plan. I knew one thing: we would not get lost…not on this mission.

# RETURN TO BARANOWICZE

As the train was approaching the city of Baranowicze, I could hear the locomotive whistles, I could see the rails splitting. My heart was beating faster and faster. I was getting nervous. Coming home was a big moment for me. I had escaped from the Baranowicze ghetto three years earlier to wage guerrilla warfare, to fight the Germans and I had done that and then some. I was wounded four times, barely surviving the last.

I had survived it all and lost my whole family.

Now I was returning home in one piece, a mature twenty year old, married to a wonderful woman and full of hope for the future.

As the train neared the station and slowed, I hugged and kissed Genia. Tears were rolling down my face.

When we got home, there was a surprise welcome party awaiting us. All our friends were there, the few schoolmates who had survived, partisan brothers and sisters and high-ranking Russian officers. My father-in-law was so excited he didn't know what to do with me. He hugged me every few minutes, telling me how happy he was to see me. It was a great party.

It took about four weeks for me to recover completely, although I was still listing slightly to the front. Having an excellent nurse and good home cooking, I healed fast and got stronger every day. With the wound closed, I could bathe and splash in a nearby lake.

After I felt well enough, one of the first things I wanted to do was go visit the place where my father worked and where he had been killed.

A Russian officer took Genia and me by jeep to Koldychevo. But when we got there, there was nothing there. It was gone. We could find no trace of it at all. The Germans had destroyed the camp and leveled the grounds. I was devastated and broke down and cried. Genia cried. Even the Russian officer, who was Jewish, cried. Silently, I thanked God Genia was there with me.

The next day we went to that part of Baranowicze where the ghetto had been.

The Jewish part of town was completely burned to the ground. There was no sign of a house or any other Jewish landmark. No trees, no grass. It was overwhelming. The town and the people I loved so much were gone – my parents, my brother, my relatives, my friends – all killed by the Germans, assisted by the local population. There were people in this town who gave the Jews up to the Germans. How could I ever look at any of them and not wonder: had that man or woman turned in someone I loved?

I did not want to live around people who hated me. The memories of the killings in the ghetto would always be in front of my eyes. On every street. Wherever I walked.

Baranowicze, the beautiful town that I once knew and loved, that I grew up in, abloom with greenery, flowers, trees and orchards, no longer existed.

I didn't want to live in Baranowicze anymore.

Genia and me at a farmhouse just prior to departing Baranowicze for Lodz, Poland August, 1945.

We never returned.

Gathering of Baranowicze survivors at the gravesite after the War, 1945. Monument on the Mass Grave where 6,200 Jewish men, women and children were murdered by the Germans. Second Slaughter September 22-29, 1942.

# EPILOGUE

The human loss of life in World War II is estimated to be 62 million people.

A few of the Jews who had managed to escape before the Germans invaded Baranowicze came back from Russia. But half the people who escaped from the Baranowicze ghetto either perished fighting the Germans as partisans in the forest or fighting the Germans with the Russian army.

All told, out of roughly 13,000 Baranowicze ghetto Jews only 250 were alive after the Russian liberation in 1944.

Captain Misha was put on trial by the Russian Military in 1945 for the murder of the three children in the forest. Many Jewish partisans spoke on his behalf. He was found not guilty, cleared of all charges and reinstated in the Russian army as a major.

The information that Samuel and the three other partisans gathered as spies in the Zorkincy partisan camp was used by the Russian military to charge and convict many gentile partisans in that camp of war crimes. They were sent to Siberia.

Returning home to Denmark after it was liberated from the Germans, the Danish Jews were welcomed with open arms by their friends and neighbors, who, they would learn, had taken care of their houses, their businesses and even their gardens while they were away.

In August 1945 Samuel and Genia and her family – her father, brother, sister-in-law and eleven other members of their "adopted" family – relocated to Lodz, Poland. In November the adopted family moved to the American-controlled sector of Germany, taking up residence on the Zetlitz *kibbutz*, less than 5 miles from the Austrian border. There coincidentally, the chief cook was Cherna Curkoff, who they hadn't seen since they left the Lipiczany Forest. Judel and Cherna were married on the *kibbutz* January 1946.

In 1946 Samuel and Genia moved to Bayreuth, Germany, and applied for visas to immigrate to the United States.

On February 11, 1949, Samuel and Genia and their two-year-old son Edward arrived in America. They lived in Newark, New Jersey, for 34 years until December 1983, when they moved to Florida.

In 1987, in the forty-third year of Samuel and Genia's marriage, Genia passed away.

Each Passover, Samuel, now 81, keeps the promise he made to himself over sixty years ago: honoring the memory of his father by not taking any bread or rolls during the High Holy Days.

After the war the Jewish part of the town of Baranowicze was rebuilt. It now flourishes as a city of 150,000, with one notable exception: there are no Jews living there. Baranowicze is *"Juden Rein."*

# AFTERWORD

I am first and foremost an American. I have loved America since the day I arrived in 1949 with my wife Genia and my son Edward. I love the freedom that America has granted me and the wonderful people who contribute to the American tapestry. I was born in Eastern Europe, in a different time. A time that served to mold my very existence. A time that is always there…with me.

I reminisce about my life often. When I am sitting in a quiet room or peaceful surroundings, I start thinking about the past.

I think about my parents, my innocent little brother Jackob, who was not given the chance to grow, and all the family I lost in the *Shoah*. My precious Lato family, murdered by the German butchers during Hitler's infamous, inhumane era in Europe.

In those still moments, I hear voices preaching to the world that the Holocaust is a lie. They say that the Holocaust never happened. They claim that the Jews fabricated the story to create sympathy for themselves.

I think, Are these people who deny the *Shoah* crazy? They must be out of their minds! They must be poisoned sick with hatred!

The only way I can fathom this is to consider that the haters, the deniers are taking advantage of the enormity, of the monstrousness that the German murderers did to the Jewish people, knowing how hard it is to believe that any "humans" are capable of such unthinkable crimes. Thus they preach that the Holocaust did not occur.

When I think back on the horror, I, myself, who lived the nightmare, have difficulty believing it…

But I witnessed these heinous crimes and with a heavy heart, I tell you they *did* occur. I have the memories and the nightmares to testify to them.

To hear the *Shoah* denied is like being tortured all over again.

I was 16 when the brutal tragedy began and I am now 81 years old.

As a survivor and as a witness I have told my story, what I went through and what I saw with my very own eyes.

I forgive, but I shall not forget!

How can I?

How can you?

After the war I tried to make sense of everything. Why did all those things that happened in the ghetto and the forest that aided me in my survival happen at just the right time, so many times? Were these miracles? Dozens and dozens of times I have found myself asking myself, Why me? Why me?

Then, when I heard voices preaching to the world that the Holocaust never happened, I understood why my life was spared so very many times – a "higher authority" wanted me to survive as a *living* witness.

For this, I have given testimony.

— Samuel Lato
April, 2006

# Lato Photo Collection

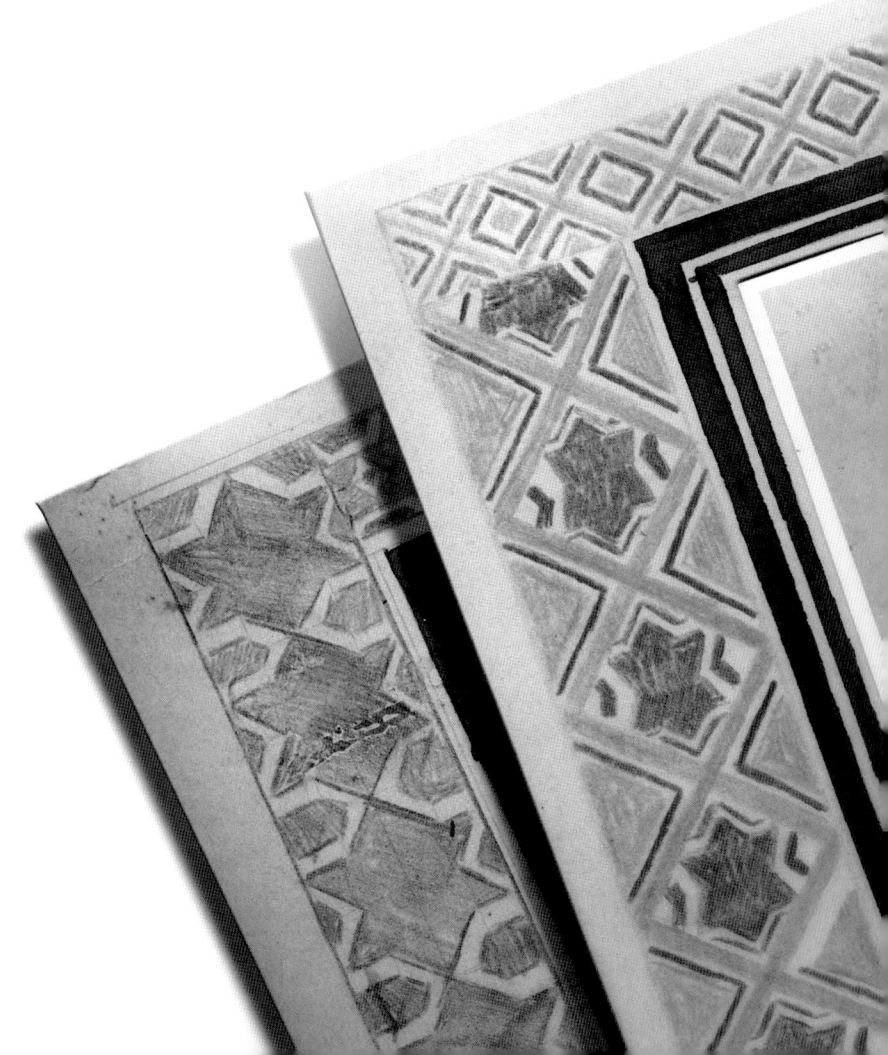

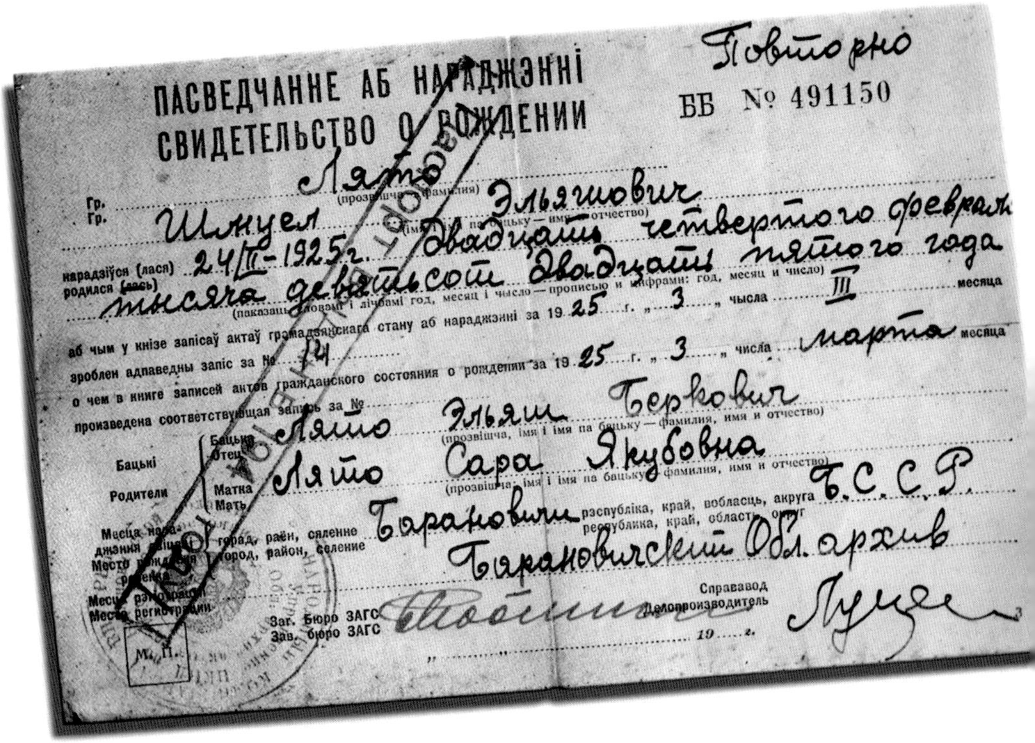
ПАСВЕДЧАННЕ АБ НАРАДЖЭННІ
СВИДЕТЕЛЬСТВО О РОЖДЕНИИ

Повторно

ББ № 491150

Гр. Лято (прозвішча — фамилия)
Гр. Шмуел Эльяшович (імя, імя па бацьку — имя, отчество)
нарадзіўся (лася) / родился (ась) 24/II-1925 г. Двадцать четвертого февраля тысяча девятьсот двадцать пятого года
(паказаць словамі і лічбамі год, месяц і число — прописью и цифрами: год, месяц и число)
аб чым у кнізе запісаў актаў грамадзянскага стану аб нараджэнні за 19 25 г. „3" числа III месяца
зроблен адпаведны запіс за № 14
о чем в книге записей актов гражданского состояния о рождении за 19 25 г. „3" числа марта месяца
произведена соответствующая запись за №

Бацькі / Родители
Бацька / Отец: Лято Эльяш Беркович (прозвішча, імя і імя па бацьку — фамилия, имя и отчество)
Матка / Мать: Лято Сара Якубовна (прозвішча, імя і імя па бацьку — фамилия, имя и отчество)

Месца нараджэння / Место рождения: Барановичи — горад, раён, сяленне / город, район, селение; Б.С.С.Р. — рэспубліка, край, вобласць, акруга / республика, край, область, округ
Барановичский Обл. архив

Месца рэгістрацыі / Место регистрации
Заг. Бюро ЗАГС / Зав. бюро ЗАГС
Справавод / Делопроизводитель
19 .... г.
М. П.

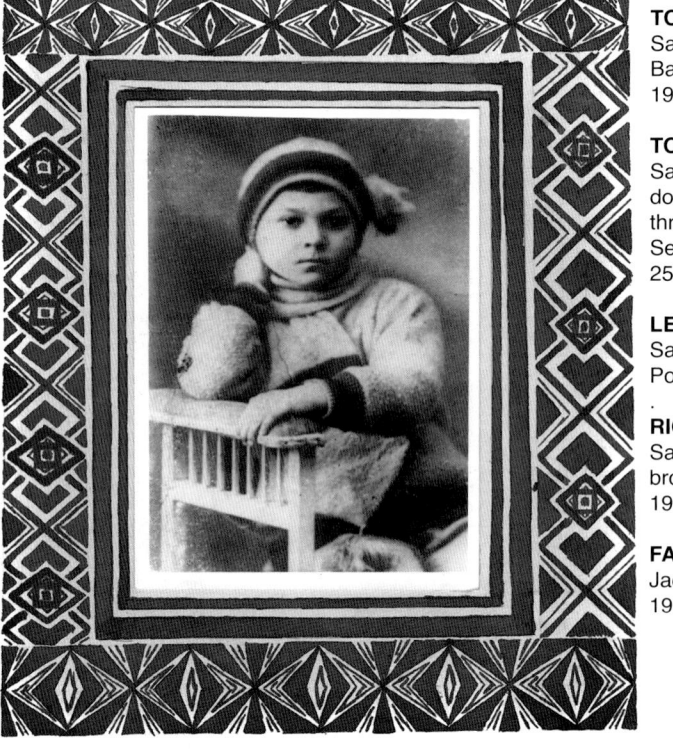

**TOP LEFT**
Samuel Lato's birth certificate, Baranowicze, February 24, 1925.

**TOP RIGHT**
Samuel Lato's student document, authorizing travel throughout Poland January to September 1939 for only 25cents, December 1938.

**LEFT**
Samuel, age 6, Warsaw, Poland 1931.

**RIGHT**
Samuel, age 10 and his little brother Jackob, Baranowicze 1935.

**FAR RIGHT**
Jackob Lato, age 3, Warsaw 1936

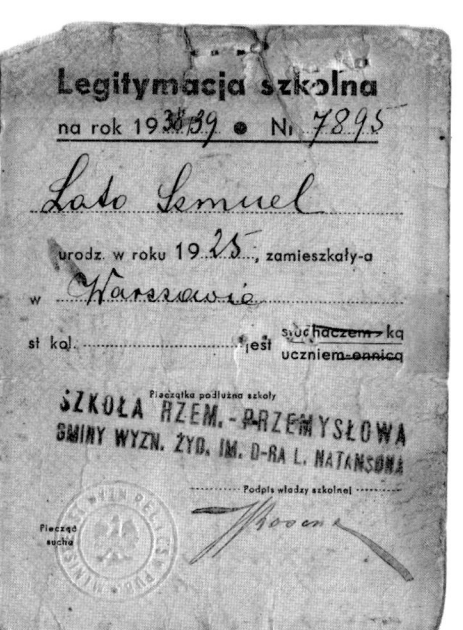

**ABOVE**
Sara Lato with cousin Elizabeth, Baranowicze 1923

**ABOVE RIGHT**
Samuel, age 3, his father Edward with his mother, Sara, and cousin Aron, Baranowicze 1928.

**RIGHT**
Grandmother Portnoff, Sara Lato's mother, 1909

**FAR RIGHT**
Samuel, age 5, Warsaw, Poland September 1930.

**LEFT**
Genia, age 13, Baranowicze 1935.

**RIGHT**
Samuel, Genia and her father Judel Wishnia with Cherna Curkoff (who later married Judel) and Max, Genia's brother, Zetlitz kibbutz, December 1945.

**BELOW**
Samuel and best friend and partisan Zalman Shuch, a few days after the Russian army liberation, July 1944.

**ABOVE**
Authorization for Genia to travel to Lodz, Poland August 1945.

**RIGHT**
Samuel Lato, photo taken from Identification card of HIAS (Hebrew Immigration Aid Society), Zetlitz kibbutz 1945.